*Dear God,
Please Get Me Off This
Merry-Go-Round and
Show Me...*

How to Respect an Irresponsible Man!

PriorityONE
publications
Detroit, MI USA

How to Respect an Irresponsible Man!
Copyright © 2001, 2004, 2025 – Updated Revised Edition Christina Dixon

All scripture quotations, unless otherwise indicated, are taken from the New King James Version®. Copyright © 1982 by Thomas Nelson, Inc. Used by permission. All rights reserved..

Scripture quotations marked (NIV) are taken from the New International Version®. NIV®. Copyright ©1973, 1978, 1984 by International Bible Society. Used by permission of Zondervan. All rights reserved.

Scripture quotations marked (AMP) are taken from the Amplified Bible, Copyright © 1954, 1958, 1962, 1964, 1965, 1987 by The Lockman Foundation. Used by permission.

Out of reverence and honor for God's Word, the word Bible is capitalized throughout this work. Also, throughout this work, the name of satan is not capitalized in order to re-emphasize Christ's victory over him.

All rights reserved. No part of this publication may be reproduced, stored in a retrieval system, or transmitted in any form or by any means – electronic, mechanical, photocopy, recording, or any other – except for brief quotations in printed reviews, without the prior permission of the publisher.

*Priority*ONE Publications, LLC
P. O. Box 361332
Grosse Pointe, MI 48236
E-mail: info@priorityonebooks.com
URL: http://www.priorityonebooks.com

ISBN 13:   978-0-970363-48-0

Edited by Patricia A. Hicks
Cover and interior design by PriorityONE Publications, LLC

Printed in the United States of America

Table of Contents

Acknowledgments i

Author's Note 2025 iii

Introduction v

1. My Story 1
2. The Dilemma 9
3. Timing Your Jump 31
4. Where Do I Go From Here? 40
5. Bug Mentality 47
6. Birds of a Feather Flock Together 57
7. Are You Really Keeping the Peace? 63
8. Don't Stop the Reaper's Sickle! 79
9. Reality [✓] Anger: Yours & His 85
10. Will the "Real" Virtuous Woman, Please Stand Up? 96
11. Just How Do You Show Respect to an Irresponsible Mate? 103
12. A Word for Wise Men: What to do When 111
13. How to Recognize an Irresponsible Man 124
14. Jump Recovery 131

Recommended Reading 141

About the Author 145

This book is explicitly written, but not exclusively, to Christ-loving women who are married to men who also profess to be lovers of Jesus. As such, the foundation for ideas presented in this publication is The Holy Bible. This book is not intended to be an exhaustive resource that answers every potential question on this issue. It is meant to encourage Christ-loving women to utilize the frustration resulting from the perpetual loss they suffer, due to patterns of irresponsibility, as an opportunity to draw closer to their Lord, who heals all wounds. The author hopes that a better understanding will promote an increase in the amount of "salt and light" these women provide their families and communities.

This publication is not intended to replace pastoral or other much-needed counseling. Although this book is explicitly written to Christ-followers, nonbelievers, or Christ-loving women whose husbands are nonbelievers, may also find this information insightful and encouraging.

Acknowledgments

To my Abba Father, my Savior, my Lifeline, my Teacher and Comforter—God. Your love, grace, mercy, and patience have generated an overwhelming sense of gratitude in my heart. Though I did not, nor can I ever earn the priceless gifts you have given, my determination to make loving You, Priority One remains.

To my husband, Michael, when I first released this book, we had weathered a mere eleven years together as we did our best to walk with God and each other. Today, having navigated even more of life's challenges for over thirty-five years, "God is STILL our Rock" as He continues to honor your words to "bless thousands of people" through the pages of this book. Your continued blessing upon this work means more than I can find words to express.

To my children, Kristina, Jason, Michael, Elayna, and Alicea, I look forward to our shared testimonies blessing families with the faith, hope, courage, and bulldog tenacity we're cultivating as we continue our journey of reconciliation.

To Mom and Dad, and my brother Samuel Alan, though you are absent from my daily life, you're yet with me.

To my sisters, Mary and Catherine, I love you. Don't ever doubt it.

To Siloam Pool, Tina Hall, Raymond Smith, Floyd Jackson, Pastor Emery Moss, Jr., and all the relatives, friends, and co-workers who were acknowledged in the original version of this work, everything I said then still holds.

May the Holy Spirit's commitment to complete the work He began in us all bring God immense glory!

Author's Note 2025

When I first wrote *How to Respect an Irresponsible Man* over two decades ago, I was in the thick of my own painful journey, wrestling with fear, loss, and the overwhelming confusion of trying to honor God while living with patterns of irresponsibility that were breaking my family apart. I never imagined that my raw, shame-filled confession would touch thousands of women who recognized their own stories in mine.

Twenty years later, women still tell me this book gives them permission to be honest about their pain, courage to set healthy boundaries, and hope that God really does see them. The biblical principles haven't changed—respect, courage, patience, and trust in God remain as vital today as they were when I first discovered them. What has changed is my confidence in sharing them. I now know with absolute certainty that the God who held me through some of my life's darkest seasons is the same God who will hold you through yours.

This edition preserves the heart of my original while making a few updates for today's readers. The core message remains: You can respect an irresponsible man without enabling his behavior. You can love him without losing yourself. You can stand on God's Word even when everything around you is falling apart. Most importantly, you can really *know*, the Father who loves you best.

If you're reading this with a heavy heart, worn down by years of unmet needs and unfulfilled promises, take courage. The nauseating cycles of loss can stop. The jump off the Merry-Go-Round is frightening, but the landing—though hard—leads to solid ground. I'm living proof. My marriage hasn't become perfect, but I have become free. And that freedom changed everything.

Welcome to this journey. May the God of all comfort meet you exactly where you are.

With love and in His grip,
Christina Dixon
Detroit, Michigan
October 2025

Introduction

The snowy white clouds in the sky looked like cotton balls playing tag as we ran to the Merry-Go-Round. We held the rails tightly as we ran around and around. My buddy said, "Now!" That's when we jumped, squealing for joy. We laughed gleefully as we went round and round. Uh – ooh! My belly was feeling queasy. I couldn't see straight. When I realized that going in circles was making me feel sick, I told my friend, "Let me off this thing!" But he was enjoying the ride. Every time the ride slowed down, he would laugh and speed it up. "I'm getting sick. I'm gonna throw up. I'm gonna jump," I cried. But I was afraid. Stay on? Jump. Stay on? Jump. What should I do? Scared to death, I prayed, "Dear God, please get me off this Merry-Go-Round!"

For what seemed like a long time, I thought about how badly it would hurt if I jumped off. We were moving awfully fast. Maybe I'd have to go to the hospital. I hoped God would make my friend consider how sick the ride was making me. But his facial expression told me he wasn't stopping. Eventually, I realized that God's answer to my prayer was not stopping my friend. He chose to answer by giving me the courage to jump.

* * *

I thought I was a kid the last time I rode a Merry-Go-Round. I was wrong. This child-like experience is a metaphor of what it is like to be married to a man who behaves irresponsibly. What begins with mutual glee inevitably becomes sickening despair. One night during a conversation, my husband said, "I don't know what it is, but you've lost something and so have I." After a couple of days of prayerful contemplation, I realized that what I had been missing was my joy. A genuine, authentic, sincere joy and gratitude permeated my life when I initially accepted Christ. Now, its consistent presence and abundant supply were gone. "Dear Lord, when did it leave? Why did it leave?" Then came the big question, "Father, how can I get it back?"

The *when* of losing my joy became clear the moment I realized that joy seeped from my heart every time I saw my husband make decisions that seemed to satisfy him, but were not in the best interest of our family. The more I focused on him and his behavior, the more miserable I became. In those moments, I not only began to lose sight of my joy, but I also lost respect for him.

There may be those reading who'd say, "She's saying it's all his fault." Though it seems that way at first glance, I am really saying that those particular instances were a catalyst in the loss of joy in my life. The real blame is mine. The operative words used earlier were "...*I focused...*"

The Word of God teaches that the work of the Holy Spirit is not only comforting, but also teaching and leading; that makes us students. As a student, one can opt to focus on the lesson being taught, look around the room at classmates, or they can focus on objects outside the window. Students choosing to focus on the lesson are much better prepared when test day comes. Classmates choosing to look around the class or out the window don't have a clue.

Many test days came in my marriage. Like a student who had not studied, I became nervous at the prospect of being tested on something I did not know. Instead of paying attention in my Life and Marriage 101 class, I had looked around the classroom at my handsome husband. As a result, I failed a lot of those tests. In fact, failure to understand and follow the guidance and leading of the Holy Spirit was at the core of my loss of joy.

In Ephesians 5:33, God instructs Christian wives to respect their husbands. Period. There are no disclaimers *(i.e., if he pays the bills, goes to work every day, loves you, and nurtures the children as the Bible says, etc.).* But how do you respect a man you believe is taking you for granted and behaving irresponsibly? How do you manage to keep yourself from "being afraid with any amazement" when your mate tells you not to pay the utility bills, or, as some have said, "Don't have the baby. Get an abortion." The Holy Spirit knew the answers and was available to tutor me; I wasn't paying attention. I was so busy looking around the classroom that when the teacher asked me a question, all I could do was tattle on my husband.

I knew I was failing at respecting my husband, and yet I wanted so much to please God. I decided to request a special class. The following months presented an incredibly challenging opportunity for me to learn more about myself, my husband, and especially my Savior. I had some very interesting sessions with my Teacher. One thing is for sure: this teacher has an unmatched ability to custom-make classes to increase student retention; hence, the analogy of the Merry-Go-Round.

As women who love Christ, if we intend to obey God's instruction to respect, as well as love our husbands *like* God loves us, our thinking must be balanced. I pray that as I share the insights obtained along my personal journey, this book will bring comfort, clarity, and a greater measure of understanding to this particular group of women, from their sovereign and loving Father – Jehovah God.

I am compelled to share some very shame-filled moments on these pages. Yet, for the joy my Father has set before me, I will despise the shame of my foolishness and disobedience and die to my self-destructive pride. May God use the foolishness of my life to confound the wise as I declare that which I have seen and heard my Father do.

Is it possible to respect a man who behaves irresponsibly? I say emphatically, "Yes!"

What happened?

1. My Story

"How's it coming with the bills?" I asked. "It's not," he answered. When I asked him what he meant, my handsome husband of seven and a half years told me that he had paid $200 on the electric bill for our dying offset printing business. "That's all?" My mind filled with a thousand questions because I knew that two weeks prior, he had completed a print job with a $2,000 tab. Surely he had done more than pay the electric bill for the print shop?

Four months prior, as we prepared to move out of our beautiful four-bedroom Tudor, which we had lost to foreclosure, my husband and I discussed our rebound strategy. He said we would live in his mother's home for three to six months. His logic was that without the expense of monthly rental payments, we would be better able to pay off past due bills *(which at the time were under $4,000)* and save for a place of our own. There are no relational difficulties with my mother-in-law. She and I have always gotten along very well. However, we run our homes very differently. Despite my many concerns, I reluctantly agreed.

A month later, my three teenagers, husband, and I moved in with his mother, three of my brother-in-law's children she had adopted, their mother, aunt, grandfather, and cousin. Yep, you counted right. Thirteen people lived in my mother-in-law's nice, but small, three-bedroom ranch. Convinced I was mostly to blame for our financial situation, my husband suggested that he handle *all* the issues concerning money. My role was simply to give him 50% of what I earned as a temp to help with *our* debts. He would make sure bills were paid and money was saved. I would have no say so. Again, I reluctantly agreed.

Here we were three months later. He had earned $2,000, and all he had to show for it was $200 on the electric bill. I forced myself to calm down and realize that he had to cover the expenses. I decided to tally the receipts for the previous two-month period. Maybe things would make a bit more sense to me. After totaling them, I discovered that though the business was "in the red," breathing its last breaths, in two months it had grossed not $2,000, but over $7,000. After subtracting expenses for the same period, I discovered that he had made a profit of approximately $3,700. That had absolutely nothing to do with the money I gave him from my earnings. As I thought about all the things my children and I were going through in my mother-in-law's home, everything in me shouted, **"I don't think so. This man is crazy!"**

When I confronted him about what I discovered, he resented my anger-laced probing. Feeling thoroughly justified, I continued to press the issue. Finally, with a "wild" look in his eyes, he told me to "Back off!" I granted his wish. Not only did I back off from the conversation. I backed off the relationship. I was determined this would be the last time I would feel like an idiot because I trusted him. Not only would he not get another dime of the money I earned, he wouldn't get anything else either! The following three years proved to be the most gut-wrenching season of my life as a Christian.

Have you ever felt foolish for trusting in your husband? If you're anything like me, you've felt that way many times. But now I was sick of it. I prayed, "Lord, help me to understand what's going on here. I know I contributed to the problem, but surely I'm not *the* problem, like my husband says. Am I?" Thus began my search to understand the dynamics of the maddening Merry-Go-Round my husband and I were on.

As I sought understanding, other women on the same journey crossed my path. We were not satisfied with the response of extremist feminism to our dilemma. In our souls was a hunger and thirst to please God. Somehow, though, it seemed His way didn't work. Could that be? Is it possible that God isn't fair? Why is He allowing this to happen to me? My husband was distancing himself from me, and the tension between us was growing. Although I spent many nights weeping bitterly, I continued to pray for understanding and relief from the frustration of it all.

Confused, dejected, yet hoping, I prayerfully began my journey reading books on marriage by various authors. Certainly, there are lots of much-needed books written to women whose husbands' lack of love and disrespect for them manifests itself in battering, substance abuse, infidelity, etc. Personally, I was amazed at how few books are written specifically for women whose husbands consistently exhibit irresponsible behavior. Yet, the Lord helped me to better understand the role I played in perpetuating the negative cycle my husband and I were in. I was challenged to face my fears by accepting and applying God's truth. Some of what I believed was error. I saw contributions I made to the disharmony in my marriage.

As I began correcting the things I was responsible for, resistance from my husband about things he was responsible for came to the surface. It wasn't long after that that I saw the connection between my confronting my husband about bills and people we owed, and his withdrawal from the relationship. Respect for him diminished with every bill collector's call, especially when he refused to hear my concerns. Oh - how much my heart ached.

I prayed, "Father, I'm still losing respect for my husband, but I love You. I want to obey You! Help me to be as patient as You are when my husband is stubborn about meeting my needs. Help me to continue being kind when my husband offends me. Help me to look beyond his faults and see his needs and continue loving him **the way You do**. I don't think I can take much more. I'm scared Mike will get angry and leave me if I show him how angry I am. I'm scared that if I leave him, my ministry will be over. Lord, what should I do?"

The book of Proverbs says, "The thing a wicked man fears shall come upon him."[1] I did not realize that when I was habitually fearful, I was being wicked. Despite having worked on fear issues many times before, it continued to rob me. I couldn't deny it anymore. I was ineffective in eliminating fear's hold on me because everything I tried only treated the symptoms. I needed to address the cause.

God's Word says, "whatever does not originate and proceed from faith is sin."[2] That means that habitual fearfulness is a form of sinfulness. I learned that fear carries seeds of marital destruction just like irresponsibility. Just as my husband needed to confess his sinful tendency toward irresponsibility, ***I needed to confess my sinful tendency toward always being afraid.*** At the root of my fear was

---

[1] Proverbs 10:24a AMP
[2] Romans 14:23b AMP

faulty thinking. I needed those faulty roots destroyed. I wanted every one of them out!

As the Holy Spirit began shining light on how fear robbed me, He empowered me to continue my Christian journey with a new set of eyes. I found new, more beneficial aspects of life to focus my faith upon. I had allowed my fear to magnify my husband's anger, instead of allowing my faith to magnify my confidence in God. I realized that my problem had less to do with my husband and more to do with my lack of courage.

It wasn't long before I began asking questions about *why* I did things the way I did. Why was I so desperate for affirmation? Why couldn't I be emotionally stable when he was moody? Why did I feel it necessary to keep him from getting upset? Why couldn't I be honest about what I really felt and thought? Scripture teaches that, "In the fear of the Lord is strong confidence and His children shall have a place of refuge."[3] If I really believed the Bible, why was I so afraid? Did I merely have a form of godliness? Was I denying His power? I lowered my defensive responses. I began to see how I *really* was, not how I imagined myself to be. Finally, I was allowing myself to be transformed by allowing my mind to be renewed. Slowly yet diligently, He began to replace fear with the light of His truth.

Only when the Holy Spirit began cleansing the bitter infection of old hurts and loved me through prayerful loving friends, who challenged me to refuse to allow the strongholds of fear to eat me alive, did I really begin to heal. Where I saw an impenetrable fortress, God saw an opportunity to teach me how to access joy, peace, and the righteousness of Christ on a completely new level in my life. Genuine heart level change began as I applied God's instruction in Matthew 7:4 to get the beam out of my own eye before attempting to remove my husband's splinter.

---

[3] Proverbs 14:26

I would love to tell you that after doing as God instructed my circumstances changed overnight. I cannot. Although it was months before my husband made what I considered to be significant changes, I changed considerably. God consistently shows Himself to be faithful, as He hastens to perform His Word.[4] I view my trials as yet another facet of His ongoing work to engrave godly character into my very soul.

Not long before I lost my home, I asked the Lord for patience. I know some of you are wincing at the thought. "Don't you know the Bible says that tribulation brings about patience?[5] Who wants tribulation?" I can assure you, definitely not me. But I do want...

- The fruit of maturity in Christ patience brings.

- To know my Savior even as I am known, not only in the fellowship of His suffering, but especially in the power of His resurrection.

- To be a person yielded to Him and moving in His Spirit.

- To be a vessel of honor, praise, and glory to His name.

- To be effective in the winning of committed souls into God's kingdom.

I don't want my faith to be merely an intellectual exercise. As valid as my current concerns are, **I believe with everything in me** that...

- God has not given me a spirit of fear, but of love, power, and a sound mind.

- They that *know* their God shall be strong and do exploits, not become the exploited.

---

[4] Jeremiah 1:12
[5] Romans 5:3

- He that began a good work in me will complete it until the day of Jesus Christ.
- My Father would not have instructed me to do something He was not willing or able to empower me to accomplish.
- My obedience regarding respecting my husband will bring glory to God.

Furthermore, I personally refuse to allow fear to threaten and annihilate my faith in God and leave me permanently wounded, miserably bitter, relentlessly angry, and eternally lost.

How'd I get here?

2. The Dilemma

As we pursue understanding the dynamics of this vicious cycle, we will look at several aspects that tend to contribute to common misconceptions involving this Merry-Go-Round. In the search for effective ways to handle difficult circumstances with their husbands, wives of men who behave irresponsibly find that customary counsel can often prove to be very ineffective. Some advise everything from being kind, to not nagging, praying, and obeying. Sometimes, after having read many books, we discover the existence of timelines regarding men's tendency to move on to the next conquest after getting married.

Even more insightful is the discovery that a great deal of men's behavior that hurts their wives is done unintentionally because they simply think differently than women do.

Relieved he wasn't really trying to hurt her, a wife in this situation often changes her expectations of her husband. She may come to recognize that she needs to become more realistic and romanticize less. Unfortunately, when you have an irresponsible person "in charge," this new information skirts around a major component in resolving the issues. Armed with hope, albeit incomplete counsel, she tries to please her husband in ineffective ways that become detrimental to the marriage. Meanwhile, the unmet needs of her family consistently fuel the gradual loss of respect for herself and her husband. Slowly, hope dies as months turn into years.

These women often subscribe to a common *miscomprehension* of scripture that frequently leads to overwhelming discouragement, resulting in an extreme lack of motivation. If nothing is done to nurture the wife emotionally, physically, and/or spiritually, a shutdown is inevitable.

The goal of many Christian wives is to emulate Proverbs 31. Hence, the desire to achieve this goal motivates scores upon scores of their decisions. "Surely if I do the things this scripture speaks of, I will please my husband, and he'll stop saying and doing things that hurt me. How wonderful it would be to hear my husband and children rise up to bless me." Subconsciously they decide that their husbands will be less aloof and more intimate if they simply give him whatever he asks for.

While a wife who deeply loves her husband may possess a desire to do everything he wants, when your mate behaves irresponsibly, it is often foolish to do so. Doing everything the man you're married to wants, how, when, and where he wants, is not synonymous with being submissive, respectful, or loving. Avoiding pain at all costs, trying to "keep him happy," isn't beneficial for the marriage, nor is it at the core of your motivation when genuinely respecting your husband.

Take a moment to pray quietly. Ask God to prepare your heart to receive the things He wants you to know. Although some of it may be difficult to hear, I pray that you will receive insight into the dynamics of Merry-Go-Round living. Better yet, I pray that you will desire to jump off the Merry-Go-Round and truly begin to live the abundant life Christ promised.

The Cause – His Contribution

The picture of family life once portrayed in shows like *The Cosby Show and Family Matters* feels out of reach for many young men today. For a variety of reasons—loss, distraction, or the challenges of life—many fathers are absent. But absence doesn't always look like an empty seat at the dinner table. In today's world, many fathers live under the same roof yet remain disengaged from the God-given responsibility of parenting. Whatever form this absence takes, the result is often the same: boys growing up under the weight of a mother striving to fulfill a calling meant for two, leaning on faith as she raises her children primarily on her own.

Unfortunately, some feel ill-equipped or are too self-absorbed to "train" or discipline their sons. Consequently, a lamentable number of absent fathers and overwhelmed mothers have sown the wind with their male children, leaving the wives of these poorly taught males to reap the whirlwind. To top it off, their poor son is wondering "what's wrong with her" as opposed to realizing "I'm missing something."

Much like characters in *Stranger Things* or *The Outsiders*, many boys today wander aimlessly—through social media, neighborhoods, or friend circles—searching for something to fill the emptiness in their hearts. Proverbs 29:15 (AMP) reminds us, "A child left undisciplined brings grief to their mother," showing that guidance, boundaries, and Godly direction are essential to shaping a young man's heart and character.

Unfortunately, as the world becomes less morally conscious, the prominence of irreverence, apathy, violence, pornography, and drugs in today's culture gives undisciplined males options that threaten to permanently distort their understanding of God, themselves, and family values.

Mature, manly involvement is a major component needed to instill a sense of responsibility in a young man's life. If no mentor is found during pre-teen and adolescent years, the longing for loving, yet firm, healthy male involvement often intensifies. Disappointment and a sense of loss soon become distorted. In some cases, a desire for mischief is substituted for a close relationship.

Mothers are often aware of their son's emotional need to see "manhood" in action. As a result, when these young men become teenagers, their mothers may attempt to fill this need by ensuring they have something constructive to do (i.e., joining a sports team or getting a job where they can earn their own money). Some get a job while they finish high school. For these young men, having been provided with a source of rewarding structure, their lives become more productive. They may even be a help to the family. In fact, hope for a healthy family life becomes an attainable goal.

Others choose the fast track and earn money by illegal means, or they work but are not taught to contribute to the needs of the family. To further compound the problem, what they do and with whom they associate is not monitored. There is little or no accountability. By failing to hold their sons accountable and requiring them to make consistent contributions to the well-being of the household while continuing to house, clothe, and feed these young men, mothers indirectly communicate that it is someone else's responsibility to take care of them. Meanwhile, they care for no one. Subjectively, a young man may believe,

"I'm a man now. I only have to do what I want to do. I'm not accountable to anyone. No one has the right to question me. If I spend all my earnings and have nothing worthwhile to show for it, that's my business. So what if the light bill doesn't get paid? Maybe I'll take care of it later. Right now I'd much rather..."

Having had little or no established training, personal discipline, or self-control, many of these men continue this pattern, completely oblivious to the reality that their lifestyle is one of irresponsibility. Typically, they seem to be unaware that the respect they desperately desire and their irresponsible behavior do not mix. For them, the problem is simple. It's their hardhearted, stubborn, and rebellious wife.

Every day in homes around America, husbands fully expect their wives to trust and respect them despite their failure to meet basic family needs. Proverbs 6:10-11 discloses the future of those who are lazy and do not work. Poverty is the consequence of their inactivity. Likewise, II Thessalonians 3:10 AMP, it is clear; *if anyone will not work, neither let him eat.* To add insult to injury, these husbands quote scriptures to their mates with great pride and conviction. With reference to the standard God has given husbands to love, provide, protect, empower, and lead their families; seldom, if ever, do they quote scripture to themselves with such fervor.

For some wives, the issue is a bit more confusing. What about the man who goes to work, but does not use his earnings to care for the needs of his family? What about those whose ability to provide is diminished by insistence upon methods of poor stewardship? His working is not the issue. The way he handles money is. The instructions in I Timothy 5:8 AMP apply here. *If anyone fails to provide for his relatives, and especially for those of his own family, he has disowned the faith [by failing to accompany it with fruits] and is worse than an unbeliever [who performs his obligation in these matters].* That means he is worse off than somebody who does not know God at all. When confronting him about poor business practices only aggravates him, what do you do then? Kill him?

Trust me, ladies, as good as that thought sounds at times, it is not the biblical thing to do. The biblical response from 1

Peter 3:3 would be to implement and maintain responsible patterns in areas where *you* make decisions. Your consistent integrity will create the kind of contrast the Holy Spirit can use to draw attention to areas where his integrity is lacking. Because many men struggling with irresponsible behavior compromise their integrity and yours, you may also need to make sure that you are not vulnerable to any negative legal repercussions. Whatever you do, don't allow his poor stewardship to become yours. *[More on that later]*

God's intent for Christian husbands as they love their wives is to provide the world with an example of the intimacy between Christ and His church. Christ's love for the church is a blueprint for a godly man. His love is described as unselfish, kind, patient, humble, yet fervent, stable, courageous, trustworthy, and just. This love further demonstrates teaching, nurturing, and protecting children. The aforementioned character traits are just the tip of the iceberg. Christ does not stop there. He empowers the church. Tyranny is not the fruit of those sincere in serving God. Its fruit is living with a person whose primary focus in life is giving his loved ones and his community a tangible example of Christ's love, grace, acceptance, equity, guidance, compassion, justice, protection, wisdom, and provision. Not for the purpose of impressing others, but out of love for his God.

An irresponsible Christian man's most effective hope of becoming a mature, balanced believer in Christ is seeing his irresponsible behavior as sin. As a "true worshipper," his response would likely be godly sorrow that leads to genuine repentance. Then, like Abraham, he can leave all that is familiar and ungodly while trusting God to lead, guide, protect, and prosper him, as he begins his personal pilgrimage to the promised land of abundant life in Christ.

For a man striving to overcome his tendency toward irresponsibility, it can be a wonderful opportunity to experience greater intimacy with God. When we *know* that God is pleased with us, leaving our comfortably familiar yet sinful ways behind, nothing compares to the confidence we gain. Pray that your mate will begin to truly trust God as he commits to the sometimes-frightening journey into the unknown.

Dear Father,
Please help my husband be a man of integrity. Like me, he is accustomed to managing things on his own. Help him to find the peace you give when we put our trust in You. Amen.

The Cause – Her Contribution

Like husbands, the wives of irresponsible husbands may or may not have had a father in the home. A girl's father, or the absence of him, sets a precedent in her understanding of male behavior. Sadly, for many women, it translates:

Face it, girl, men are stubborn and seldom change. Expect them to hold you to a higher standard than they are willing to live by. Expect a separate set of standards for him that does not include fairness, honesty, or intimacy.

If he is going to be in your life, it will be on his terms. All your pleading will do is drive him away. If you choose to pursue your dreams, you may find him pursuing someone else. If he decides to ignore your needs, take it all in stride. Take it or leave it, girlie, 'cause if you want a man in your life, this is it!

Alas, what she sees every day is on a collision course with her dreams. Many young girls spend much time fantasizing about how different the man they marry will be from the men they've seen growing up. In fact, many times they subconsciously determine that their husband will be like the diligent, yet charming prince in Cinderella or Sleeping Beauty. After absorbing these conflicting lessons, along comes a potential husband. He is kind, attentive, and gentle. Maybe he's adventuresome and full of charisma. Just so he's nothing like her absent or unavailable father. She falls in love. She may compromise her integrity by giving this man her affection before the appointed time. But what does it matter? She believes they really *will* be married soon. Some young women go through this process several times, repeating the same mistakes simply because they never deal with the vacuum created by never being accepted as the valuable divine creations of God they are.

After what feels like an eternity, the big wedding day arrives with little to no counseling at all. Some get married filled with joy, hope, and anticipation. Some get married even though their hearts and minds are filled with questions and apprehension. Nevertheless, happy to be married, she expects all her fantasies and dreams to come true. Instead, reality sets in. As soon as her husband feels the honeymoon is over, BOOM! Suddenly, she feels like Belle in the animated classic, "Beauty and the Beast." Only she isn't sure whether her husband is cast as the "Beast" or "Gaston." He no longer treats her like the delicate flower he once prized. Now she feels more like the weed missed by the lawn mower. They used to talk for hours. Now he barely speaks to her at all. Unlike his pattern during courtship, he doesn't seem to care about what she needs. Now he acts as though she is his maid. He doesn't have the same desire to *be with her*. In her insecurity, she thinks, *"What did I do wrong?"* The painful realization of rejection takes a deeper foothold. She slowly becomes convinced that something is wrong *with her.*

Convinced her husband's distance is somehow her fault, she desperately seeks the return of the intimacy, attention, and tenderness that marked the courtship. She tries to initiate communication. He lets her know one way or another that he's not interested. The pursuit/rejection cycle begins. Round and round and round we go, where we'll stop nobody knows. "God, please get me off this Merry-Go-Round!"

With no real information from him, she begins to make a more conscious effort to pray while seeking to obey God's Word. However, her perception of what that truly means is frequently distorted. Armed with misbelief and a determination to salvage her marriage, she begins planting in the soil her mother-in-law tilled. In reality, she becomes a manipulator, an appeaser, or worse, she could become a desperate, insecure woman who says no to the liberty of God's truth because she is too afraid to say yes to the good things faith in Christ offers. The underlying cry of the heart becomes...

"Please don't stop loving me! What you want and how you want it are most important. I should have never tried to show you your insensitive, irresponsible behavior toward those you profess to love. I should have kept the peace." "Maybe if I try harder to be a better wife, he'll come around." Or, "Whatever you say, just don't be displeased with me."

Different woman. Same problem. No accountability. No limits. No reason to consider anyone else's needs or feelings other than his own. Inevitably, it only serves to worsen the condition of her husband. The more you do for him, the less he appreciates it. The more you ask of him, the more he hates it. Caught in a vicious cycle of offenses and disappointments, they go round and round. It's not long before it all begins to take its toll.

If no relief is given to the wife, who counselors agree is generally the first to seek resolution of their problems, hope fades into frustration, which gives way to anger, anger to despair, and onward into hopelessness, hopelessness into hardness of heart, and in numerous cases, hardness of heart into divorce.

> *"Lord, how can he throw Your word at me when he isn't obeying You himself? Win him without the word? Are You telling me that I can't ask questions about our future or what's happening with the money? If not me, Lord, then who? Surely this is not what You meant?!"*

Like David, wives are asking, *"Is there not a cause?"*[6]

Though there is most definitely "a cause," it is the responsibility of Christ-loving women to seek understanding from God and, if necessary, repent. The tendency toward fearfulness and an attitude that *demands* a husband to be loving and responsible is sin. It is very unlike Christ to demand our husbands' love and provision. God does not demand that we love Him.

For others, fear is the obstacle that keeps them from confronting their husbands about serious issues. Their mates' approval is valued more highly than their desire to *do* the Word of God. Although this reality is generally hidden, once uncovered, it reveals how little the truth of the Holy Spirit is understood.

I like what my husband shared with me once. He said that God told him, "Mike, you and I don't always agree. But, I'm always right." As difficult as it is to accept at times, our response to life's harshness is often misguided. Such is the case when we choose unbiblical ways of responding to our husband's irresponsible behavior. Take a look at the list below. Are you on the Merry-Go-Round because *the* truth has been replaced by...

- Unhealthy concern about how things look as opposed to how they really are?

---

[6] I Samuel 17:29

- The deceitful calm of "keeping the peace" when no genuine peace exists?
- Failure to communicate how the loss you've suffered is affecting you?
- Avoiding or denying the harsh reality of imperfect human nature?
- Masking *true* feelings with out-and-out lies or sugar coating?
- Attempts to control the uncontrollable?

These are just a few of the unbiblical responses wives may have when interacting with a husband who behaves irresponsibly. Because these responses do not have confidence in Christ as their core motivation, they feed the vicious cycle I call "The Merry-Go-Round."

The Cause – The Church's Contribution

> *"So I returned, and considered all the oppressions that are done under the sun: and behold the tears of such as were oppressed, and they had no comforter; and on the side of their oppressors there was power; but they had no comforter. Ecclesiastes 4:1*

Thank God more churches are speaking out against domestic violence and various types of mental and emotional abuse perpetrated by men upon women and children. May He bless those who reach out to women and children whose bodies, hearts, and minds are battered by violence and blatant abuse of authority.

However, the harm experienced by family members as a result of irresponsible and neglectful behavior is much more evasive and less visible, thus it is not addressed as readily. In stark contrast, biblical culture shows that it was completely unacceptable for a man not to take care of the basic needs of his family. Sadly, in many churches, teaching men the importance of accepting and fulfilling their responsibilities is sorely lacking, while the wives' duties are heavily emphasized.

Traditionalists often tend to dismiss women who tell anyone about their husband's behavior as carnal and disloyal. There seems to be very little concern for women whose faith in Christ, love, and joy are slowly being choked out by a perpetual state of loss and neglect. As is often true in relationships of this type, wives pray that someone in the body of Christ, filled with God's Spirit, will discern their silent suffering. For them, the comfort that scripture says "members of the body" ought to extend to one another is lacking.[7] Instead of ministering encouragement and hope, church leaders often indirectly condemn her for "complaining."

Some husbands and church leaders who profess to be disciples of Christ are quick to quote their wives, 1 Samuel 15:22-23 KJV, which says that rebelliousness "is as the sin of witchcraft." It's ridiculous how justified these men can tend to feel in their stubbornness. This is despite the fact that the rest of this very scripture says, "stubbornness is as iniquity and idolatry." Determined that they don't *need* counseling, they refuse to seek help with their family problems.

In some circles, a disapproving posture is shown toward any believer who would seek relief and counsel through a psychologist. To be sure, there are those in the field who scorn the faith of their patients. But let's not discount the benefits to be obtained through counsel founded upon balanced biblical principles.

If a woman is unable to have anyone really listen to her concerns in the church she attends, where then is she to go? Too often, because leaders lack practical insight, the pat

---

[7] II Corinthians 12:14-26

answer is, "to God." The compassion and consistent demonstration regarding the Lord's instruction to us to love one another, bear one another's burdens,[8] And build each other up in our most holy faith seems all but forgotten.

Matthew 18 instructs an offended person to make the offender aware of the offense between the two of them, alone. If repentance is not forthcoming, the Scripture teaches the offended party to return to the offender with one or two others, so that in the mouth of two or three witnesses every word may be established. If the offender refuses to hear wise counsel from the one or two, the offended one and the witnesses are instructed to bring it to the church. If the offender refuses to listen to the church, believers are instructed to treat the offender as one who not only does not know Christ but also is in rebellion against Him.

However, pastors are seldom willing to make themselves available as a witness between a husband and wife, much less an instrument of God's justice, by instructing church members to no longer receive an unrepentant husband as a member in right standing with God. Church leaders appear to have concluded that the scripture in Matthew 18 does not apply to circumstances involving marriage, as they are considered "private."

At some point, there needs to be consistency concerning awareness and practical responses when assisting couples where the man *(who the Bible says is to be the head of the home)* is the irresponsible mate. To be sure, there are many irresponsible wives, but in homes where biblical values are upheld, a woman's irresponsibility does not seem to greatly disturb church leaders' sense of what should be the "traditional norm".

Sin in the church would be significantly reduced were believers to actually practice bringing other God fearing

---

[8] Galatians 6:2

believers into moments of consistently unresolved offenses. The instruction from scripture would allow...

- *Meek spirited* intervention that would communicate that both parties are loved and *their* best interest are at heart. Yet it would be clear that God's truth is loved more.

- In this meek, spirited manner, witnesses would prayerfully intervene for the purpose of holding the viewpoint of each person involved up to the light of God's truth.

- Because God's Word cuts through to the very intent of man's heart, it could be determined which person(s) involved are being drawn away from God by the lust of their own eyes, flesh, and pride of life.

- If no authentic repentance were evident after the *meek spirited involvement* of the witnesses and the church, no question would remain about the resistant person's lack of sincerity in following Christ.

- In which case, the Body of Believers would stand firm on the foundation of God's Word as they release the disobedient one into the hands of the Lord, but out of their fellowship.

Reluctant to confront their husbands, it seems that some church leaders find it easier to teach wives that it is not *their place to confront their husbands*. Though there are women in the church who would relish an opportunity to *set their husbands straight,* women sincere in their desire to please God, *want* to respect their husbands. In fact, they would welcome additional accountability in the form of mature, well-respected, Spirit-filled church leadership where someone their husband respects would address him with the thorny issue of responsibility, Christian man to Christian man. Not only would someone else see how irresponsible her husband is, but it would also confirm that she isn't crazy for wanting to keep the baby, pay the bills, or get the children shoes that fit. Better still, they would love for their husbands to realize that their confrontation is not a rebellious act, but a loving one.

When listening to some pastors preach or teach about how wives need to handle problems with their husbands, it puts me in remembrance of the guests of Ahasuerus after Vashti refused to display herself before them, in the book of Esther.[9] *(An excellent example, by the way, of a time a wife shouldn't do as her husband asks. More on that later.)* At times, there seems to be more concern about the potential implications and their impact on their personal relationships with their wives than about rightly dividing God's truth.

Some men speak highly of the necessity of accountability while simultaneously exemplifying carte blanche decision-making. As a result, the reality of God's Word being profitable for reproof, rebuke, and instruction is being diluted. If I genuinely love you, but I say nothing when you are in disobedience, I am assisting you in the continuation of your sin. The opportunity for you to rise to the challenge of really living by God's truth and experiencing His love is lost, and I am also accountable.[10]

The Bible's clear instructions to husbands regarding treating their wives as *joint heirs in Christ* seem to be at odds with *common comprehension* of what it means to be the "head of the house." Husbands who behave irresponsibly often abuse family members in their role as "head of the house" by *controlling* their loved ones. At times, wives are frustrated when their husbands seem to communicate that they want them to respond as children instead of adult partners. Adults think for themselves, form their own

---

[9] Esther 1:9-12
[10] Ezekiel 33:6

opinions, and make their own choices about what they want and don't want in their lives, don't they? You bet they do.

In many cases, when wives choose to stand upon the Word of God with their irresponsible husbands, church leaders choose to remain uninvolved or committed to a distorted view of the chain of command. If you've tried the pastor, the bishop, and the church mothers and no one is willing or able to provide effective help, then what?

To add insult to injury, Christian husbands who shirk their responsibilities to their spouse and/or family are even allowed to continue holding positions of leadership in the church. Even some pastors' wives are experiencing perpetual loss in their families due to their husbands' irresponsible behavior. Who do you go to for spiritual guidance when your husband is your pastor and you have problems with him?

When you realize that you and your husband are unable to communicate and resolve issues effectively, you should be able to seek the assistance of church leadership, where tenderness and compassion are extended, and the matter isn't dropped because someone refuses to face facts. Many Christian marriages are still in trouble because church leaders don't follow up.

Having tried God's way only to get no relief, wives often become filled with despair. After a while, all they seem to have the strength to do is go to work, come home, and mumble words to the kids, maybe read, pray, and go to bed. Activities previously viewed as impossible to live without suddenly become expendable. Seeing how ineffectively God's servants carry out His instructions, they begin to lose hope. Slowly, they eliminate church related activities from their lives.

When your life is *breaking down* right before your very eyes, and it seems your brothers and sisters in Christ don't care enough to get their hands dirty by getting involved and offering effective help, you wonder, where is the love Christ said we should show one another? If you're a church leader reading this, pray and ask the Lord what your role should be in matters like this. When He begins to show you couples in your congregation that you've neglected, let Him show you how to approach things. He knows just how to meet people where they are. Remember, He looks beyond our faults and sees the *real* needs of people.

There is yet another contribution church leaders add to this vicious cycle that I'd like to discuss. I'm talking about the lack of healthy, balanced, godly examples for young women in the church. The Bible teaches that older women *in the Body* are to teach the younger. Unfortunately, in many churches, the older women are not wiser for their experiences. In many cases, they are often very bitter and unwise.

I recall a conversation with an older Christian woman doing the demonstration of a new voter's booth procedure. She boldly declared herself an advocate of abortion. After stating that I didn't believe God would accept a woman's self-centered career pursuit as an appropriate justification for taking a life via abortion, she said that in church settings where she is a prominent leader, she encourages "prevention" of unwanted pregnancy. Although I understood that this woman's view was based on the harsh realities she'd witnessed, her original declaration made it very difficult for me to respect her as an older woman in the church. I must agree that children experience a great deal of suffering when they have mothers who don't want them. Nevertheless, as women of God, it is our duty to uphold God's truth at all times, not our personal opinions based on our meager, finite points of view.

Sometimes, the examples younger women in the church see aren't that blatant. There are also examples of older women who have resigned themselves to being their husband's doormat. As such, their example is one of fearful emptiness. Young females, who have been raised in a culture filled with satan's lies and extreme feminist views, are often turned off by what they see as the "doormat" role. It has the potential to leave them with the impression that God is not only unfair, but He is against women.

Church leaders, who discern the tactics of the enemy regarding this issue, are to be commended for their efforts to change things according to God's design. However, that change is slow coming. Christian families are suffering from the effects of divorce and abuse at the same rate as non-Christian families. At some point, these issues must be given even greater priority in the church body. Church leaders need to examine their responsibility to bring a greater measure of balance to the message of liberty in Christ with regard to married believers. To be sure, a great deal of wisdom from the Holy Spirit is required. A Christian husband struggling with being consistently responsible may find it frightening to realize that his wife is – FREE. As an adult, she has the same liberty to make her own choices as he does. She is also free to suffer the consequences of her actions just as he is. As believers *in Christ,* the exercise of this liberty is even more profound. In fact, it is a believer's Spirit-ordained responsibility and privilege in Christ to stand firmly upon the Word of God.

When one spouse stands on the Word of God and the other operates in the lust of their flesh and eyes, along with the pride of life, it inevitably generates antagonistic moments in a marriage. Part of the responsibility God has given church leaders is to build up and encourage those standing upon God's Word and to lovingly correct and reprove those who profess Christ, but do not live to please and obey Him.

For these things to happen, the church must consistently practice a willingness to get involved by following scriptural instruction. Partially because Christian leaders fail to take loving biblical action, *Christian* husbands who justify their irresponsible behavior continue in their pride and stubbornness, despite their wives' continued prayers. Someone needs to lovingly challenge their husbands to live a Christlike life while letting them know that their irresponsible behavior is sin.

The Cause – Society's Contribution

In American culture, distorted views of love and liberty, coupled with the failure of followers of Christ to stand for Him by modeling godly principles, seem to have produced a bumper crop of irresponsible folk. As a result, moral famine is spreading like a disease across our country. For centuries, history has taught women that "boys will be boys." Consequently, many women believe there is no such thing as a man who is able to nurture a woman's personhood while continuing to provide her with loving leadership and protection. Sadly, many of us have no frame of reference. When it comes to what we recall, too many only remember someone who was tyrannical or absent. Sure, there are pleasant memories. However, for the majority, consistency only manifested itself in terms of dominance or lack of involvement—the response - feminism.

As I understand it, the feminist movement began decades ago with noble goals. The denial of women's right to vote, own property, equal pay for equal work, as well as the exposure and hopeful elimination of sexist behavior against women, often hindered females in their pursuit to develop their own God given potential as persons. Unfortunately, what began as a legitimate stand against the injustices women suffered at the hands of wicked male sin nature has also been tainted by the wickedness of female sin nature.

The dictionary defines feminism[11] as the theory of social, political, and economic equality of the sexes. It further defines liberation as the act or process of striving for equal rights and status. In many cases, those objectives have been accomplished. Although men are still paid more for the same work, women now have the same opportunity as men in this country to vote and own property. Ailments suffered by women, once thought to be "imagined" under male medical care, are now receiving highly improved care due to women adding new insights in the medical field as physicians. Our presence in the multitude of workplaces has made a remarkable impact on the amount and level of service provided in various businesses, contributing to the nation's economy at large.

Unfortunately, for some, the noble goals of the movement's original pioneers have been used as an opportunity to demand the right to become as selfish, greedy, insensitive, power-mongering, irresponsible, and murderous as many men.

For women who desire to live Christlike lives, equality of the sexes is obtained through genuine faith in Christ and application of God's Word. There is nothing more liberating than truly knowing, receiving, and acting on God's truth. God's Word says that when we *know* the truth, that truth will *make* us free.[12] Believers have been passive in living out their faith too long. As a result, society lacks a clear understanding of the authenticity of God's power as a whole.

In the minds of many women who have suffered consistently and unreasonably, there is little or no difference between male dominance and male leadership. Sadly, men in the church have not sprinkled enough of the saltiness of God's design in their relationships with their wives to demonstrate before society that God's will *really is* perfect

---

[11] Webster's New Collegiate Dictionary, © 2001.
[12] John 8:31-32

and acceptable. Spousal and child abuse happen frequently in the homes of "saints" and "sinners" alike. Therefore, unbelievers often view our faith as unrealistic and unfair. For many, it is merely a way to subjugate those at a disadvantage – specifically, women.

What if communities around the world at large could see men who love Christ consistently loving and leading their families, working on their jobs, in their churches and communities, with the servant's heart of Christ? What if hardcore feminists could see intelligent, emotionally healthy, courageous, Christ-loving women who are growing personally and spiritually, willing to respect and submit to the leadership of their husbands? Surely the contrast between satan's bondage in the life of an unbeliever and God's peace and liberty in the life of a believer would generate an awesome ground swell of hunger and thirst for a relationship with God in the souls of the lost. Instead, the removal of the Ten Commandments from courthouses, unhealthy sexual behavior, freedom to kill unborn children on demand, and rebellion against authority are among the perverted battle cries of our day.

Dear Father,

As I become familiar with many of the things that may have contributed to the heart-wrenching losses my husband and I have experienced, I realize that this is just one step in the process of preparing myself to jump away from the vicious cycle we're in. Help me not to use any of the information You've led me to uncover as justification for not respecting my husband when I believe his behavior to be irresponsible. Don't allow me to distort this information so I can use it as a weapon in disagreements with my mate. Instead, help me to see opportunities to grow closer to You as I consider the contributing factors that got our lives in such a mess. Thank you for Your faithfulness to us both. More and more, I'm realizing how much we need You. Amen.

3. Timing Your Jump

1. To every thing there is a season, and a time to every purpose under the heaven:
2. A time to be born, and a time to die; a time to plant and a time to pluck up that which was planted,
3. A time to kill, and a time to heal, a time to break down and a time to build up.
4. A time to weep, and a time to laugh; a time to mourn, and a time to dance;
5. A time to cast away stones, and a time to gather stones together, a time to embrace and a time to refrain from embracing,
6. A time to get and time to lose; a time to keep and a time to cast away;

7. *A time to rend, and a time to sew; a time to keep silence, and a time to speak,*

8. *A time to love, and a time to hate; a time of war and a time of peace.   Ecclesiastes 3:1-8*

    As you read the above scripture, please pay close attention to its balance. The imbalance and bondage of emotionally unhealthy behavior can be seen more clearly when held up to this light. It is unrealistic to insist that every "time" in our lives be times of birth, harvest, healing, building, gathering, embracing, receiving, keeping, mending, silence, loving, and peace. Seldom do we want to face the planting, breaking, weeping, mourning, casting, refraining, losing, rending, speaking, hating, and war-filled moments of life. Though we view the latter with negativity, they are a necessary part of life. If one truly lives their life, they will experience all these things.

    When applying this scriptural reality to our lives, we are faced with what could be a frightening question. What time is it for me? Could it be that I am in a time of breaking down or weeping? Could it be a time of mourning for me because I've been losing? As a wife and mother, the breakdown of family relations has been extremely unsettling. At times, I've felt that I would stop the earth's revolution *(if it were possible)* in order to stop the breakdown and loss I saw spreading in my family. When we witness the decline of our husband's ability to relate to us and others in a healthy way, our entire being seems to yell, "Nooooooooo!!" Our response to this feeling is to "fix" things as quickly and as best as we can. The thought of simply letting things break down is unacceptable.

    However, verse 3 says, "there is a time to break down." Let's look specifically at a time to plant. Without breaking, there is no planting or harvesting. The ground must first be broken in order to receive the seed. The seed must be broken in order for the stalk to come up. The stalk must break in order for the flower to bud. The flower must die to make way for the fruit. When the fruit is eaten, it must be broken with the teeth. Once in the stomach, it continues to be broken down until its nutrients can be absorbed into the body. At each stage in the process, a state of change or brokenness must occur. Even Christ's body was *broken* in order for us to receive remission of our sins.

I recall moments of intense intimacy with God where I cried out, "Do whatever You want with me, Lord!" However, when He wanted to break down my unhealthy patterns and responses, I recoiled, "satan! The Lord rebuke you!" Little did I know it wasn't satan at all. God was answering my prayer.

I am reminded of the New Testament scripture where Jesus broke the bread at the Passover.[13] He told the disciples that the bread was His body, which was broken for us. We were to do this in remembrance of Him. I've often wondered if He was speaking merely of remembering Him by participating in The Lord's Supper, as is the custom in many churches. Could it be that He was instructing His disciples to allow themselves to be broken? I'm not referring to physical brokenness. The brokenness I am speaking of is a willingness to trust God's Sovereignty in our lives when things we hold dear are breaking down right before our very eyes.

It could be that you aren't in a breaking time. Maybe it is time for you to *refrain from embracing.* In an attempt to demonstrate our love, many times we embrace the unhealthy and ungodly behavior of others. I am reminded of several wives and mothers that I know who allow their sons and husbands to treat their home like a revolving door. In their 30s and 40s, these men have never been able to consistently maintain a home, a relationship, or life on their

---

[13] I Corinthians 6

own. They bounce from one woman's house to another, never accepting responsibility for their lives. Yet they are quick to tell anyone who "disrespects" them that they are – a man. If this is the case in your life, you may need to learn how to refrain from embracing. To embrace something means to welcome it.[14]

Those I know personally who love irresponsible men may be afraid and/or confused. Still, they are definitely not consciously welcoming the heartache and pain they experience as they embrace the unhealthy, irresponsible behavior of men they love.

You may be thinking, Christina, I *have* to embrace my husband. The Merry-Go-Round I'm on is going fast. I have to hold on tight, or I'll be seriously injured. How can I let go when I know flying off this thing could kill me? My dear sister, trust in the Lord with all your heart. Don't lean on your own understanding. In all your ways acknowledge Him, and He will direct your path, Proverbs 3:5-6.

Several years ago, during a devotional word study, I discovered that one of the meanings of the word **trust** is *to allow something without fear of the consequences.* [15]

When you stop making excuses for your mate and begin allowing him to experience the consequences of his choices, it can get really scary. What kind of wife will people think you are? Will they see you as disloyal, lazy, and selfish? When you decide to stop nagging your mate about spending time with you and the children, the reality of how little he wants to be with you can be heartbreaking.

Can you trust God with your brokenness? How do you respond when your husband can't get the car or other "toy" that he wants without your signing on the dotted line? You

---

[14]Merriam-Webster, I. 1996, c1993. *Merriam-Webster's collegiate dictionary.* Includes index. (10th ed.). Merriam-Webster: Springfield, Mass., U.S.A.
[15]Merriam-Webster, I. 1996, c1993. *Merriam-Webster's collegiate dictionary.* Includes index. (10th ed.). Merriam-Webster: Springfield, Mass., U.S.A.

know it's beyond your family's means. You also know that he tends to say or do *nice* things because he wants something. Later, when the rubber of responsibility meets the road, you will be the one stuck with the bill collectors. You know his license is suspended. Why do you allow yourself to ride along when he is driving? What about when he expects you to sign the joint tax return despite the fact that you don't have a clue as to what's going on or how he finagled such a large refund? What will you do? Will you trust God and stand for what you know is right, or will you decide to give in to your husband's childish antics by pacifying him?

Jesus said, "Let not your heart be troubled."[16] The word *let* implies that you have a choice. You can either continue to be troubled in your heart while pacifying your mate or choose to trust God. As you prepare to take this *jump*, timing *is* crucial. A leap at the wrong time or for the wrong reasons could cause unnecessary, avoidable damage. But God's Word still applies.

Remember, this is a work that you have committed to the Lord. Not only is God more than able to finish what He started, but He said that when we commit our way to Him, He will establish our very thoughts.[17]

Have you been manipulating, appeasing, or complying for so long that you have actually been "training" your mate to believe he can almost always get his way? Even at the cost of your and your children's faith and self-respect? Do you want to train your daughters to expect the same ungodly misery you're enduring? Do you want your sons to repeat the same unhealthy patterns with their wives? If you were appearing before the judgment seat of Christ so that you could receive what is due you for the things that you have done in your body, good and bad, and God asked you, "Why

---

[16] John 14:1
[17] Proverbs 16:3

did you help my son continue to disobey Me?" What would you say? "Lord, I was scared!?"

In the parable of the talents, the one who did nothing with his talent said it was because he was afraid. The Lord's response was to cast him into outer darkness and give what he had to someone else. Surely you don't want this to happen to you. But you will need to count the cost. Make sure that you are willing to suffer the agony of changing for the abundant life in Christ you say you want.

Certainly, you will experience fearful, anxious moments. Jumping off of something that is moving can be frightening. Absolutely, you will make mistakes. Yes, this process will hurt. But remember, lady, our God isn't pleased with fear-filled responses. Believe it or not, if you are repenting of *your* sinful acts and grieving the losses you've suffered, you are right on schedule. It's time to jump off this sickening ride. Take courage and allow the spirit of God to...

- *Pluck up* the weeds of pacifying behavior that have been planted.

- *Break down* the strongholds of fear.

- Help us *mourn* losses we may suffer.

- *Cast away* the stones of control and manipulation.

- Tell us what we must *refrain from embracing*.

- *Rend our hearts* from unhealthy confidence in our ungodly ways.

- Teach us the wisdom of discerning when and what to speak.

- Cause us to *hate what God hates* and love what God loves.

- Go to spiritual war so that we may experience *a time of genuine peace.*

Dear Father,

*I need so desperately to be in the timing of Your will. As I consider my circumstances, help me to keep my eyes focused on You. I want to walk in the Spirit so I won't fulfill the lusts of my flesh. I know I can't do this without You. I lift my life up to You. It is such a broken mess. But I **know** You can fix it.*

Now what?

4. Where Do I Go From Here?

When focusing on the passing view while riding a Merry-Go-Round, after a few revolutions, the ride is so nauseating that it's almost intolerable. Only when the focus is on the people riding with you does the reality that you're not going anywhere cease to be nauseating. But you're not enjoying this ride. You feel trapped. You feel sick. You want off this contraption!

The illustration of a Merry-Go-Round communicates the futility of what I call the pursuit/rejection cycle. The more you pursue your mate to address the serious problems you are facing, the more he rejects confrontation and runs from reality. Driven to resolve issues, you pursue and confront. Unaccustomed to working through problems, he flees and rejects. As the cycle continues, nothing ever gets resolved, and the relationship goes nowhere.

Looking outside the Merry-Go-Round, we see the abundant life of Christ promised whizzing by. We sense God's desire for an intimate relationship with us as His children. In our hearts, we know He wants our relationship with Him to extend beyond coming to Christ. He wants us to experience the liberty and acceptance that come from being *in* Christ. We hear the beckoning of the Holy Spirit to allow Him to *transform* us into the image of the Father's dear Son.[18] However, the very essence of transformation is change. To the Lord's dismay, change is something His people resist tooth and nail. We find acceptance of the status quo much easier.

However, one must be mindful to *receive* the truth for God's transforming power to manifest itself in our lives. In fact, it is in our best interest to transform *(change)*, not who we are, but *how* we are. The Merry-Go-Round has us in bondage when Christ has already given us freedom. It drains us of energy when the Lord's joy has been given for strength. It brings chaos when the fruit of God's Spirit brings peace. John 8:31-32 says, "If you continue in My word, then you are My disciples indeed; and you shall know the truth and the truth shall *make* you free." In order to make the transition from a state of bondage into a state of liberty, we need to *know* the truth. King David said, "Behold, you desire truth in the inner being; make me therefore to know wisdom in my inmost heart" Psalm 51:6 AMP.

The Holy Spirit has as one of His prime directives to lead and guide us into all truth. In fact, one of His names is The Spirit of Truth.[19] Sadly, the truth often hurts. The word "hurt" conjures up an array of painful images in all of us. Ironically, human nature tends to run from anything that will cause it pain. It doesn't matter to us that it may be

---

[18] Romans 8:29
[19] John 14:17

beneficial. All we know is that hurt is painful. As far as we are concerned, anything that hurts is bad.

As the Holy Spirit leads and guides us, we may recall painful memories. He will not only show us where others failed us. He will also show us where we failed others. He will help us to accept our need to leave some things behind. Much like the Hebrews had to leave the familiar, convenient things of Egypt *(which, by the way, they longed for when their journey got tough)*, so will we. How can we enter the Promised Land of abundant life in Christ if we refuse to exodus the binding and destructive though familiar and convenient methods of our past?

The question is, "How are <u>you</u> *really* doing?" The phrase, "How are you?" has become a courteous thing to ask while continuing on your way. Seldom does anyone sincerely want to know the answer. But the Holy Spirit is still asking the question. Unfortunately, the answer for an incredible number of women is, "I feel broken. Fragmented. Torn." These are the feelings that provide the pain that motivates us to change. Let's expose this pain to the light of God's love and truth.

Let's begin our "jump" by accepting the reality that there is absolutely nothing wrong with being a submissive wife and wise mother. As women who love and follow Christ, our families are to be our top priority. When you jump off this Merry-Go-Round, you will not be leaving your marriage; to the contrary. You will be jumping away from the vicious cycle of loss and unresolved problems into the secure foundation of faith and trust in God and His faithfulness. The balanced thinking, courage, and emotional stability you gain through this *process* will be an instrument God can use to save and restore your marriage.

As lovers of Christ, we want the benefits that come from having men in our lives who are willing to be accountable and submit to a holy, righteous God. But too often, we are afraid to stand in faith. There are those in our self-centered culture who would say, "Do you really expect us to believe that our husbands are really going to stop abusing, neglecting, and abandoning our families? They haven't so far. Are you saying we should trash all the progress women have made via the feminist movement and risk returning to the dark ages? You've gone stark raving mad! You know very well men will see our efforts to respect our mates as an opportunity to dominate women!"

The issue isn't whether or not there will be those who will twist and turn the truth to obtain their own selfish ends. In all honesty, the imperfect, rebellious nature of humanity will more or less provide us with those who will choose the easy path of selfishness. Nor is the issue whether or not we will return to the inequitable days of yesteryear.

Certainly, the *evil* that has caused a lack of consistent, loving involvement from our husbands is potent. It is a major cog in the cycle of division, indifference, and dysfunction. It *is alarmingly common* in marital and family relationships around our cities, towns, and villages. It is not new. It *has been robbing families* for centuries. If our husbands are unable (or unwilling) to muster the courage to go into the battle to save our families, where the destructive forces of satan are robbing us blind, then who? The answer, ladies – we are. The God we've surrendered our lives to is our General and Commander-in-Chief. Defeat is not an option.

As I've spoken to women married to men who behave irresponsibly, they have expressed an inward fragmentation that works against the wholeness and liberty that faith in Christ promises to bring. The contrast between what the Lord promised and what our experience is may cause many women to feel "emotionally nauseated." For the purpose of this book, we'll define emotional nausea as agreement on the outside while spirit and mind, will and emotions are in a tumultuous storm of disagreement on the inside. *Emotional nausea* is caused by the inability to reconcile "earned" respect with the harsh realities of irresponsibility and its fruit *(i.e., guilt, shame, unmet basic and emotional needs, emotional, verbal, and physical abuse, etc.)*

Irresponsibility brings with it many aspects of suffering. Fear, poverty, shame, loss, anger, frustration, and neglect are but a few on the list. For some, the losses have been so many that grief has become a constant companion. Before you can recover one loss, another presents itself. The experience of perpetual loss may have you beginning to wonder, "Where is the abundant life Christ promised? Surely when the Lord said we'd be troubled on every side, He didn't mean this! Did He?!"

Does the Creator of the heavens and the earth have the ability, desire, and willingness to answer the sincere heart cries of hundreds of thousands of men and women around this country who want His will in their lives? The answer is an emphatic **YES!!!**

Living with a fearful, resentful, or rebellious attitude is not godly. Should we respect our mates is not the issue. If we are going to obey our Lord and Savior Jesus Christ, we *must* respect them. In fact, women who strive to be biblical in their responses to life are to be commended for their willingness to defer to God's plan. But we must first understand what the word respect really means. Webster says that the act of respecting someone means that you are considering them worthy of high regard and esteem. [20] At the heart of respect is the consideration of value and worth.

As followers of Christ, we believe that all human beings are priceless. Why else would Jesus have paid the ultimate price of His life to redeem us from sin? How often do you look at your mate and ask God to help you see him as one He loves? [*Yesterday? It's possible, but I doubt it.* ☺] While our

---
[20] Ibid

mate's behavior may cause us to feel like they are not worthy of our respect or consideration, that doesn't mean that they lack precious value. Having said that, are you willing to acknowledge that because God chose to make mankind in His image,[21] He didn't make junk when He made the man you love? Can you accept the implications of that truth?

Your husband's worth is **not** determined by his behavior. It is determined by the value placed upon him by his Creator. The same is true of you. As wives, we are very wrong to attempt to devalue one Christ loves. Webster also says that the (1560) *transitive verb* of respect means *to refrain from interfering with.*[22] Oh, how we love interfering.

Being "salt and light" in the world as Christ followers, we should have a quality about us that preserves (in this case, *preserving our marriages and families)* and illuminates. That means we can "light up" our husbands' lives by our lifestyle, while remembering that there *is* a difference between influence and interference. Expect that you'll be in some dark places during this process. Otherwise, lights aren't needed. ☺

Dear Father,
Thanks for reminding me that my husband's value is not diminished by his behavior, any more than the value of a priceless jewel is diminished by its being buried in the mud. Help me to see that my mate, like a buried jewel, may be buried in sin. Yet still he is worthy of high regard and esteem. I'm wrong to allow his behavior to be a reason to devalue him. Help me to keep in mind that he is a soul for whom Christ died.

Lord, help me not intrude unasked and unnecessarily into areas in my husband's life where I have no right or power to change or control things. Help me to recognize that to do so is to interfere with areas of his

---

[21] Genesis 1:26
[22] Ibid

life that are matters concerning the condition of his heart, which You see much more clearly than I do.

I can't always tell the difference between interfering and influencing. Please help me realize that any lasting positive effect I may have will be due to the presence of your Spirit dwelling in me, not any direct efforts on my part. Amen.

5. Bug Mentality

Scripture says that if we endure times of suffering, we will reign with Him.[23] As you examine your life and the irresponsible behavior of your mate, you may be overwhelmed by the suffering you've experienced. Up to this point, your suffering has been merely the consequence of your and your mate's actions or failure to act. As you seek to obey our Lord by respecting your mate, you will discover that your suffering will take on new meaning. It will no longer be a consequential experience. It will become a tool in the hand of a loving God, a catalyst in maturing the fruit of His Spirit in your heart.

Be prepared for inward resistance. You may find that each time you decide to change, you experience resistance in your heart. You want to know the truth, but somehow you don't seem to want to hear it. Eventually, you may have to face the reality that although God loves you, you don't love

---

[23] II Timothy 2:12

Him as much as you wanted to believe, and all your flesh really wants is the benefits that come from serving Christ. You have no desire to suffer at all, for any reason. But your genuine love for Him will allow the Holy Spirit to reveal the strength of your tendency to cover up shameful thoughts and actions. Somehow, in the midst of this process, He gives you a desire to embrace the truth about you. Not your mate. Not anyone else. Just you – and Him.

As I underwent this part of the process, I asked the Holy Spirit to give me an understanding that would help to create a desire for His truth within me. In other words, "Lord, give me what I need so I can stop being afraid to look at the truth about myself." His answer came in the form of a memory. Some of you may find it repulsive. But you will also find it effective.

It was 1978. I was 18, a mother of one with another baby on the way, and no husband. Unwilling to "make" the father of my children marry me, I had to move out of my parents' home. It was perfect, I thought. The landlord gave me the five-cent tour of her available 4th-floor, one-bedroom apartment. Only five blocks from my parents' Motor City flat, I could have my cake and eat it too. Mom was close by if I needed her, which I always did. I was also within walking distance of grocery shopping and bus lines. With no car, that was perfect. I couldn't wait to move in.

I checked the cabinets, closets, and water pressure for any signs of landlord neglect and found none. With the $250 per month rental charge, I informed the landlord that I was ready to pay the first month's rent and security deposit so I could move in immediately.

The freshly painted walls and recently sanded hardwood floors that had been coated with varnish and buffed to a high gloss effectively masked the truth. Little did I know that the entire apartment building was home to a huge infestation of roaches. It took me about two or three months to realize that the pesky vermin were actually the real owners of the building.

During the two years I lived there, I would learn that it didn't matter how much I exterminated my apartment. There was little hope of having a roach-free place to live if the owner didn't take care of the entire building.

I believe roaches are one of God's visual aids for His "Hidden Evil and Its Characteristics 101" class. I know this sounds disgusting, and for some of you, it may be offensive. Nevertheless, it illustrates the futility of not dealing with the unpleasant truths about why we continue destructive behavior.

I once spoke with an exterminator who told me a lot about these repulsive bugs. Roaches have a 30-day breeding cycle that makes it very difficult to annihilate them. When left unchecked, roaches can effectively spread germs and various diseases. They thrive in places where darkness, decay, and filth abound. They detest light, and to our dismay, they are also very resilient. Any dirty dishes left in the sink or food on the stove provides a food source for these pests. What you exterminate your home with today may possibly not affect its unhatched offspring, leaving a new generation of roaches immune to what their parents encountered. If an entire dwelling place is not completely exterminated, they will simply move from one room or apartment to another. There is speculation that roaches would probably be able to survive a nuclear blast.

When having your home exterminated effectively, you generally commit to a 12-month process. You are instructed to empty all your cabinets, cupboards, closets, and dressers. Shelf paper has to be removed and the shelving thoroughly cleaned. What a mess! Then the exterminator starts leaving pesticide in the basement and works his way up to the top floor. After that, the exterminator returns once a month until the contract's final month. The necessity of consistent cleanliness during and after this process is vital in the prevention of any further infestation.

Like roaches, the evil in our hearts detests the light of God's truth. It runs to hide the second His light shows up. It is unfortunate in our "cosmetic age" that we are more concerned with how things look than how things really are. We want so much to be accepted by others, especially in the church. We put on well-designed masks. For countless people in the Body of Christ, church services are merely a weekly masquerade ball they attend. We hide behind smiles, hugs, handshakes, and quaint "God bless you" greetings.

Underneath is quite another story. Pain and frustration, guilt and shame are rarely allowed to show themselves. The deceitfulness of this ritual is the perfect breeding ground for evil in our hearts. As we learn what things don't get us our way, the self-centered evil in our hearts pursues other means of satisfaction. When our ineffective, ungodly behavior is exposed by the truth, like bugs, we tend to run for the dark, decaying shelter of denial, manipulation, appeasement, or tyranny *(to name just a few)*.

The dark, dismal, decaying thought life of an unloved, neglected wife, coupled with little or no communication, is the perfect breeding ground for evil to spread its debilitating diseases. One day, it's merely a curt remark. Weeks later, it's a full-blown argument filled with attacks upon each other's tender sense of self-worth.

For the wife who has allowed her thoughts to breed roach-like manifestations of manipulation, pacifying, stubbornness, indifference, or hypocrisy, the idea of making your husband aware of his offenses brings great anxiety. Afraid to confront, some wives would rather take their frustration out on their children than address the *real* issues. Others choose to invest all the love into their children or personal interests. Anything is better than changing again only to obtain temporary relief. The ways women come up with to protect themselves and cope with their husbands' irresponsibility are endless.

What about you? Has communication with your spouse been decaying for some time? Does the man who claims to love you take his time paying the bills? Does the man who believes he's "the boss" have trouble obeying his "Boss?" When talking about things that are important to you, he says he doesn't care. What are your thoughts about him? *[Be honest.]*

The dwelling place of faith, joy, and hope inside a wife's heart can become like a home infested with roaches. The waste and disease of doubt and hopelessness, maybe even hate, intensifies. The love, peace, joy, and courage we should possess as a result of knowing Christ are missing in action.

There is a way that seems right, but it is the way that leads to death.[24] Not your husband, honey, *you*! Sure, he *is* going the way that seems right to him. But what can you do about him? Nothing. The only one you can really control is yourself. Here-to-fore, you have been going the way that seems right to you. Have you been experiencing death? For some, the love in your heart for your husband is being choked out. Due to a lack of nurturing, it is dying. Even worse, some are experiencing the slow death of their faith. More and more, it seems illogical to believe that God really cares or that He is just. We think, "God, why did you decide that the very ones who can't seem to handle *any*thing get to run *every*thing?"

For a long time, those were my sentiments exactly. The ways "that seemed right" in my own eyes were choking the life out of my faith and liberty in Christ. I was operating in the instability of emotional understanding. I was willing to do almost anything to stay out of certain types of pain. Despite all the changes I earnestly sought to make over the years, *I still needed to allow Him to change **me**.* Once again, God's light exposed – me.

---

[24] Proverbs 14:12

The Holy Spirit would not permit me to continue avoiding the truth about my tendency to justify maintaining a state of fearfulness. In essence, He put His foot down with me and said, "No more cringing at raised voices—no more defensive yelling. No more pretending not to care to protect yourself. No more being out of control. No more manipulating circumstances to avoid conflict. Christ's behavior is your example of how to speak the truth in love and stand firm. No more running. No more being driven by fearing loss of relationships. No more cynical masks. No more losing heart or faith. Your Heavenly Father establishes limits in relationships with others. So should you. You asked me to get you off this Merry-Go-Round. I will. But you must take courage and follow the instructions I have given you."

How do you exterminate the bugs of hopelessness and despair in your marriage? I like to tell the story of a young couple who had begun to see roaches in their home. One night during a conversation, the husband left for the kitchen to get something to drink. Once he turned on the kitchen light, he saw several roaches. He quickly grabbed the fly swatter and began swatting them as fast as he could. After a few seconds, he cleared the kitchen of any visible signs of the pests. Wondering what was taking him so long, his wife went to find him. There he was in the kitchen with an intense look on his face, armed with the swatter like a soldier holds a loaded gun when surrounded in enemy territory. He was determined to swat anything that moved. Smiling, she said, "Surely you don't plan to get them all tonight, do you?"

As humorous as that little story may be, that husband's approach to the problem is an excellent analogy of how we try to approach the elimination of serious issues in our hearts. By standing ready to swat any ungodly thing that stirs in our hearts, we lose the "rest" we could be receiving from God. How ineffective. In the upcoming days, weeks, months, and years, remember that you are not the exterminator of ungodly "pests" in your life; God is. He has the most effective methods for ridding the human heart of its deceitful wickedness. Certainly, you have the responsibility of cooperating with the Holy Spirit when He brings things to your attention. However, Philippians 1:6 says that He that began a good work in you will complete it unto the day of Jesus Christ. Please note that it is "a work that *He is doing*." That work is described as "good." One of the most glorious things that will become apparent as you commit yourself to this process is the reality and potency of God's love and mercy *for you*. In fact, before you were born, He knew about every "bug" you would uncover. Yet, He still loves you. You've been loved all along. You have *never* been alone. He has always been there, waiting to share His love with you. Your heart will be overwhelmed with amazement as you realize how much He truly loves *you*. His Word is true. Where sin does abound, His grace does much more abound.[25]

There are no instant remedies for learning how to regain the respect you once had for your mate. As stated earlier, this is a process. Because scripture instructs us to count up the cost before taking up our cross, I want to share what costs jumping off your Merry-Go-Round will include:

- Repenting of your lack of confidence in God.
- Grieving over the emotional hurt and loss you've suffered.
- Deciding to change you *only*.
- Embracing God's love and grace daily.
- Refraining from your "contribution" to unhealthy cycles.
- Accepting your husband as he is.
- Taking courage from God to respond biblically.

---

[25] Romans 5:20

- Commitment   to the process.

In the following chapters, we will look at some of the *truths* about relationships with irresponsible patterns. When the truth shines upon you, exposing your weakness and failure to respond biblically in your marriage, I pray remembrance of the "parable of the roaches" will cause your old behavior patterns to repulse you. Refuse to scurry away like a roach. Be honest with yourself and God. Allow your sin to be exposed in the light of God's love. Know that all that displeases Him will be changed as you bask in His brilliance. There is no need to stand all night ready to swat the evil in your life. The lover of your soul has the ability to thoroughly cleanse the "bugs of evil" in your heart. Eventually, you will be able to speak the truth in love to your mate. Call upon the exterminator of evil, the Lord God of Heaven, who is your Father.

Repentance – Standing Naked in the Brilliant Light of Truth!

As you begin removing things from the shelves of our hearts so that God's light and righteousness can thoroughly cleanse us, we find it can be emotionally strenuous work. Nevertheless, it is eternally worthwhile. In orthodox Christian faith, it is foundational that the heart of mankind possesses an evil nature that tends toward rebellion against God. This evil is too resilient to be slothful about this part of the process. As you yield yourself to the leading of the Holy Spirit, you will become aware of the destruction and havoc your personal wickedness has caused and perpetuated. *(i.e., child neglect, domestic violence, murder, infidelity, stealing, hatred, substance abuse, attempted suicide, etc.)*

Undoubtedly, you will experience moments of intense sorrow.

I like to refer to these moments as *standing naked in the brilliant light of truth.* This nakedness reveals the existence of a great gulf between God and the realization of how grossly ineffective our personal efforts are. God's holiness is the *brilliant light* that causes us to see our need to change. His love, mercy, and forgiveness cause a hunger and thirst to ensue. The resulting decision to turn away from evil is called – repentance.

True repentance yields changed lives. Christ's power brings the willing heart through the above process and into the place where we welcome a relationship with Him and accept the reality of how much we, as fallible, finite creations, need to depend upon His infinite, infallible wisdom and guidance.

Take a moment to think about God Almighty looking beyond the multitude of your faults so your unmet need for love, acceptance, wisdom, and empowerment can be met. Does it evoke intense gratitude?

For me personally, the gratitude was so intense that I was compelled to promise Him that I would do whatever He said to do and go wherever He said to go. Little did I know that one of the first places He'd send me was into the painful battle between my evil desires, satan's lies, and His truth, in my own heart.

As I continued to look at the mess I was on the inside, I was forced over and over to stick with my initial decision to obey Him. Many times, my love for Him was being tested. Some days, I wondered what in the world He expected from me. I am so thankful that the Holy Spirit has been the Helper God said He is. I desperately needed His help to stick with my decision when the novelty wore off and the reality that I still had to suffer the repercussions for my actions became evident. God is not mocked; whatever you sow, that is what you will reap.[26]

As you consider jumping off your Merry-Go-Round you will need to *decide* to…

1. Stay under the light of God's truth in His word.
2. Stay focused on His commitment to *your* heart's inward condition.
3. Continue to trust Him, no matter how hard it gets. In the end, it will all be worth it.

Dear Heavenly Father,

In this moment, I may not realize how much I respond to the light of Your truth like a bug fleeing to the safety of the darkness in my heart. But You know. As you show me truths about myself that I may have sensed, denied, avoided, or just plain been ignorant of, please help me to respond like Your beloved and not like a bug.

Thank you for allowing me to see that running from the truth keeps me from true intimacy with You. Please expose the ways I hide from the light of Your truth. I have blamed You, the church, and most often my husband. To place all the blame for my problems somewhere else is to hide like a roach. I am not a bug. You created me in Your image, for Your pleasure. I have buried what You've given me under masks. I've used those masks as protection too long.

As my Refuge and Creator, You really do know what is best for me. It is a much wiser choice to put my trust in You. Your Word tells me that "He who covers his sin shall not prosper." Lord I want to "prosper, even as my soul prospers." Father prosper my soul. Sanctify me by Your word of Truth. How desperately I need Your grace, patience and mercy as I surrender myself to You while beginning the process of really changing. In Jesus' name, Amen.

---

[26] Galatians 6:7

6. Birds of a Feather Flock Together

One of the truths you may need to face is that, though opposites attract, many times people are drawn to those who are *like* them in some way. You also need to accept the fact that all of the irresponsible behavior in your family does not fall on your husband's shoulders.

Because a woman's need for security is so great, she may be more responsible than her husband is when it comes to paying the bills. After all, if there is no gas or electricity, her sense of security is threatened. However great our need for security, it does not exempt us from making irresponsible choices.

I recall wanting a flower arrangement to accent the dining room of my house. It cost me over $100 to have it made to fit the color scheme of the room. In looking back, I realized that at the same time some of my children had outgrown or worn out their school shoes. How did they feel when they had to wear worn or outgrown gym shoes to school and I was decorating the house? Having talked with them, I discovered my irresponsible behavior often communicated that *things* were more important to me than they were.

If I had been asked, "What's more important to you, how your house looks or your children having adequate school clothes?" there is no doubt in my mind that I would've said, "That's a dumb question! The needs of my children are much more important." But that is not what my behavior said. To my shame, I must admit that my behavior was irresponsible.

My irresponsibility did not stop there. As the Holy Spirit honored my desire to be transformed into the image of His Dear Son, I had to face the harsh reality that there were many times when my choices did not communicate love and concern for my children's needs *at all*. To make matters worse, I was just as guilty as my husband when it came to being passive with regard to certain obligations. In fact, in an effort to keep my husband from "living off me," I chose not to get another job when our family business began to fail.

Because he felt that I had more marketable skills, my husband suggested I should work another job to keep us from losing our home. Meanwhile, he would go to our failing business and service any customers that *might* walk in. To me that looked too much like his doing nothing while I did everything. My attitude was *"If he wants all the authority, he should have the responsibility to go along with it."*

I decided to *wait* for customers at our failing business with him. Initially, I believed that God would "light a fire under him" and remind him that a man is supposed to support his family. It wasn't until after God didn't step in and we lost our home that I realized that for my children's sake, I really should have gotten a job. I had only been thinking about myself. My only concern was keeping myself from being *mis-used*. I ended up feeling more than used. I felt like an idiot. What was I thinking? How could I have been so stupid? Meanwhile, we lost the business and our beautiful four-bedroom home that had appreciated $30,000 in value in less than 5 years.

But wait. What about my irresponsibility as a mother with regard to allowing my husband to abuse my children emotionally? In an effort to maintain a "united front," I sided with my husband at times when his discipline was excessive or unwarranted. At times, I suspected he may have been taking his frustrations about our finances out on the kids, but I never got up the courage to let him know how concerned I really was. I was too afraid the fury would come my way.

During those times I prayed a lot. But I never really did anything. Listen ladies prayer is always appropriate. God's Word instructs us to pray without ceasing. However, for some Christians "prayer" is merely another way of procrastinating. At times that is what prayer was for me.

I have since talked with my children and *invited them* to share how the pain of those moments impacted them. After listening to their hurt, I asked their forgiveness for my remaining silent and allowing my husband to use corporal punishment at times when, in fact, the punishment didn't fit the crime or no *crime* was committed at all.

The reality of *my* irresponsibility was obvious. Yes, God would hold my husband accountable for his irresponsible behavior, but He would hold me accountable too. I asked God's forgiveness but it was a long time before I could really receive it. I thought after I came to Christ that blatant foolishness would be absent from my life. But fear of confronting my husband and concern over whether I could really handle his being angry opened the door for torment and it hindered me from taking much needed action.

If you are experiencing similar circumstances, take time now to repent. Repent of confidence in your way of doing things. God is merciful *(full of mercy)*. He knows you are only trying to protect yourself. Trust that He really does know best. Give yourself permission and time to grieve over the losses you are experiencing due to *your* failure to respond appropriately. Do not allow satan to deceive you into placing all the blame on your husband. When the Holy Spirit leads, permit those you may have hurt the opportunity to share their hurts *about things you did*. Grieve with them over the losses they may have suffered. Give them time to heal. Acknowledge your irresponsible contributions to their loss. Realize that the things you are going through can help you accept how desperately you need Christ. Surrender your desire to *look like* things are okay. Ask Him to strengthen, settle, and establish you. He will help you love your husband, children, and others in a balanced way. To every thing there is a season. This may be your time to mourn. Our Lord said, "Blessed are they that mourn, for they shall be comforted."[27] Trust that He will see to it that you receive the comfort you need.

Dear Father,

Help me to stop looking at my husband's failures and start looking at myself. Help me to take the log out of my eyes first. I am ashamed of the irresponsible things I have done. I have been condemning my husband for not taking appropriate action and I have been just as guilty as he is.

You said that whatever I sow that's what I will reap. Some of the losses I have suffered up to this point have been the harvest of doing things my

---

[27] Matthew 5:4

own way. Your ways are right and just. Too often mine are inconsistent and, therefore, unreliable.

*Thank you so much for guiding and comforting me through this difficult time. As I prepare to talk with others (my mate, children, siblings, parents, etc.) about how **my** behavior may have affected them, give me courage to face the fruit of my poor choices. I am afraid. But, I am encouraged by the knowledge that You are with me. Help me rest in the knowledge that as I go through this season of mourning, You will comfort me by Your Spirit. Amen.*

7. Are You Really Keeping the Peace?

Pacifying, manipulating, and avoiding are methods you may have used that *you can change*. To accept what you cannot change, while changing what you can as you receive wisdom in discerning the difference brings serenity *(peace)*. Having accepted that we can only change *our* behavior, not our mate's, we need to continue to receive *(embrace)* the courage to change the things that we can.

"I didn't say anything because I was trying to *keep the peace*" is a phrase a wife often uses when she has a tradition of avoiding the pain of her husband's possible rejection or anger. It is amazing how little peace is actually *kept*[28] in those situations.

Ask yourself, "Is there an absence of hostility in my heart and in my relationship with my mate? Have we agreed to end our hostilities? Are we having harmonious relations? Do I feel secure in the relationship? Can I acknowledge that if the bills aren't getting paid there is an absence of order? If any or all of the above is painfully absent, where is the inner contentment and serenity I am keeping?" Sadly ladies, an awful lot of the time, there is none.

Though the phrase *keep one's peace* found in the dictionary means *to be silent,* we are challenged, by virtue of the process we're in, to *examine why* we keep silent. Is it out of loving, inspired obedience to God? Or is it out of fear of our husbands' response? Much of the time we keep silent we are avoiding pain because we are afraid. We will do almost anything to stop our husband from hurting our feelings. We even pacify him when we know it isn't in his best interest to give him what he wants.

For a long time this was true of me. I was a woman desperate for approval, love, and affirmation on the inside while being bold and confrontational on the outside. Can you imagine how confusing my behavior must have been for my husband? One day I was confident that his lax way of paying

---

[28] Webster defines *keep* as: 1. To retain possession of. 2. To have as a supply. 3. To provide with maintenance and support. When you "keep the peace" are you filled with resentment, anger and frustration? Does your stomach seem to boil inside? Let's look at the definition of *peace*. 1. The absence of war or other hostilities. 2. An agreement of treaty to end hostilities. 3. Freedom from quarrels and disagreement: harmonious relations. 4. Public security and order. 5. Inner contentment: serenity.

bills, etc. was important enough to risk further loss of intimacy by confronting him. The next day I wanted him to bathe me in reassurance that he still loved me, which due to his lack of understanding at the time, he was not likely to do.

Needless to say, we went; round and round. Somewhere along the way, his talking to me, showing me affection and attention became more important to me than standing firm on God's Word. Somehow, I came to believe that I had to please everyone. If I suspected that I had displeased someone, my heart would become filled with anxiety. I would try to find out if in fact I had offended someone and if so, when and how. I was driven to make things right. "What can I do for you to *like* me again?" Somehow I became convinced that loving meant *always* being available and showing *respect* meant *always* saying, "Yes." That behavior seemed so godly to me. I just knew I was pleasing God. The truth was, underneath the surface my fear cried out,

"Please don't be mad at me. Ple-e-ase don't walk out on me!"

Maybe you haven't pacified your husband. Maybe your problem is one of becoming absorbed into him so much that you don't even know what you like and dislike anymore. You might even be the woman whose response is to manipulate her husband into doing the right thing. Remember that you do not have the ability to change your husband.

To demand someone demonstrate their love is to rob God's Word of its intended impact on the lives of others. Love's power is more potent and effective when loving responses come from a willing heart. The minute we feel that we *will* get what we want from our husbands, we are not being loving toward them because love does not demand its own way. Yet just as many husbands demand their wives' respect, wives are demanding their husbands' love.

Out of the fervency of His love for us, God is challenging us to face truth, change, and truly serve Him. Out of the love

God has placed in your heart for your mate, choose to stand firm against ungodly behavior. As women desiring oneness in our marriages, we may have a tendency to *pretend* to be loving and respectful in order to get our husband to *do the right thing.* Seemingly respectful acts are not demonstrations of love. More often than not they are reluctant resignation. This is not the example Christ left us. His example is one of balanced grace and truth. Ask the Holy Spirit to show you how to balance the truths you are discovering with His grace.

For some of us, we will need to learn how to say "no" to ungodly behavior and confront without attacking. Still others will need to learn how to say things once and cast it upon the Lord, while resisting the urge to nag. Others will need to take off the mask, speak up, and let their husbands know what is going on with them. At times the Holy Spirit may lead you to do all these things. In any case, there is no textbook that will give you a specific method for each circumstance. You will simply have to spend time with God. Listen to Him for instructions on what and how to do things one step, one day at a time.[29] Because you are human, you will have moments when you will fall. But God's love and the love of those He will send will help you get up and try again as you courageously recommit to the process and remain determined to go through.

Authentic peace has always been available to those who trust God. As a "Fruit of the Spirit," peace is an outgrowth of being connected to Christ, the True Vine. *Keeping peace* can be accomplished in the truest sense of the word when you understand what peace is and how God intended us to obtain it. If in your life "keeping the peace" has meant avoiding needed confrontation, accept the reality that avoidance isn't keeping peace – it is cowardice.

---

[29] Luke 11:9

God desires His people to be givers and receivers of His love, acceptance, godly counsel, and accountability. These things cause relationships to thrive. Without healthy, balanced relationships where all these things can be expressed the masquerade within the Body of Christ goes on indefinitely. This completely disregards the Lord's instruction in II Thessalonians 3:10-15 and I Timothy 5:8.

For even when we were with you this we commanded you that if any would not work neither should he eat. For we hear that there are some which walk among you disorderly working not at all but are busy bodies. Now them that are such we command and exhort by our Lord Jesus Christ that with quietness they work and eat their own bread. But ye brethren be not weary in well doing. And if any man obey not our word by this epistle **note that man and have no company with him.** *That he may be ashamed. Yet count him not as an enemy, but admonish him as a brother. Now the Lord of peace Himself give you peace always by all means the Lord be with you all.*

and

But if any provide not for his own, and especially those of his own house, he hath denied the faith and is worse than an infidel.

By following God's instruction to not count him as an enemy but admonish him as a brother, we are expressing love as we stand on the firm foundation of His Word. The problem is, how do you reconcile not keeping company with the one you're married to and living with?

The first step is to *note* those who are disobedient. This requires us to be honest about what we see. Too often we choose to deny the reality of what we see. Denial of irresponsible patterns may help us to avoid the pain of confrontation but it does not alleviate the problem. In order to turn from irresponsibility toward responsible living, we must be honest with ourselves about the role we play in helping our mates continue in darkness about his irresponsible behavior patterns.

Taking notice of unhealthy patterns is a major step in positioning yourself to jump off the Merry-Go-Round. As for *keeping no company* with those who are disobedient, do not assume that you will be leaving the relationship. For some that may eventually have to be the case, but initially you will only be leaving the irresponsible patterns *you* have. Consequently, it will leave your mate to spin in vicious cycles - without you. Merry-Go-Rounds are simply no fun when you are riding alone.

It may be awhile before your mate realizes you are serious. That's why it is important during the process to be as consistent as possible in establishing your own personal stability and standing firm in your commitment to God and His word.

I discovered that what many of us call standing firm on God's Word is really being stubborn in the name of Jesus. In order to uncover whether you are standing firm on the Word of God, or merely being obstinate, ask yourself these questions: "What is at the core of my firmness? Am I harmfully determined not to be misused? Mistreated? Taken for granted? Am I free from the need to follow through on revenge-filled thoughts? Am I confident in the knowledge that God loves my mate best and that He has committed Himself to finishing the work He started?

Spend time with God. Let Him reveal the honest truth. It is foolish for women who are beloved of God to continue unhealthy, ineffective, sin-filled cycles. To do so is to communicate by our actions that we believe our way of doing things is more effective than God's. By doing things God's way, we demonstrate our love for Him. When we refuse to do things His way then, quite frankly, we are in sin.

When times get unbearable, you may have to simply "rest" in our Father's lap as the storm rages outside. He won't scold us for being afraid of the noisy thunder and lightening of our circumstances. Nor will He refuse to let us feel safe in His arms. Because His name is our strong tower, when we run in to Him, He will smile at our confidence that He can calm our fears and keep us safe. [30]

Sapphira No More!

The New Testament contains an example of a woman we **do not** want to imitate. This woman's name is Sapphira. In Acts 5:1-11 this woman and her husband, Ananias, initially vowed to give the proceeds from the sale of property they owned to the church. However, they later decided to give less than what they first vowed, and hold a portion back for themselves. When Ananias entered the temple giving his gift, he gave the offering deceitfully.

However, he was not prepared to stand in the brilliant light of God's holiness. The Holy Spirit revealed to the apostle Peter what Ananias was doing. Upon having his deceitfulness exposed, Ananias fell dead before the congregation. Some time later, Sapphira entered. When asked if she and her husband made such and such an amount on the sale of their property to give in the offering, Sapphira chose to lie. The apostle Peter then let her know that she and her husband hadn't lied to men but to God. He then had the same men who carried out her dead husband come to retrieve her corpse also. There is a consequence to a wife following her husband into sin. Blaming her husband will not alleviate the penalty or consequence of sin.

Sapphira had a choice. She did not have to agree with her husband by lying about the amount of money they made. When Peter asked her about the money, she could have chosen to tell the truth. Had she told the truth, she would have been a widow, but she would not have been dead.

---

[30] Proverbs 18:10

How differently would their lives have been had she noted her husband's deceit and refused to be in agreement with him? How differently will your future be? This scriptural account of Sapphira is a warning to Christ-loving women. Do not be deceived. It is foolish to follow your husband into sin. But why on earth would a Christian woman follow her husband into sin?

Often times a woman will follow her husband into sin because she has never understood that you could leave a person in their behavior, without leaving them. Sometimes women are afraid of the emotional suffering that will inevitably follow. Some of us remember how hard it was when we initially accepted Christ. We may have wanted those we cared about to come to Christ with us, but they refused. When they noticed the change in our attitude toward the things we used to do, the people we associated with spoke evil of us. In some cases, they even attempted to punish us.

It is an emotionally painful thing to know you've done what is best only to have those you love ridicule your efforts. Likewise, as you consistently separate yourself from the vicious cycle you and your mate have been in, he will be tempted to make life uncomfortable for you.

As discussed earlier, when a person stands on the Word of God, the light of God's truth exposes that which is not right. His light not only exposes you, it also exposes those in relationship with you. As you willingly accept what God shows you about your own faults, you find yourself less determined to seek justice for the things you've suffered. Because you have become more familiar with your need for mercy, you will find compassion for your husband increasing when he resists hearing the truth, just like you did. Because you understand the struggle with accepting truth, you are more able to trust God for the patience loving your mate will require during this time.

As you begin to practice "speaking the truth in love" to your mate, the resistance you encounter may be similar to what Moses faced with the Pharaoh. In the first place, you haven't successfully and consistently opposed his behavior before. As far as he is concerned, why should it be any different now? He may not yet understand that he has been resisting the ways of God. In the second place, he may not believe you are speaking the truth or separating yourself from his behavior out of obedience to God's Word. In fact, your obedience to scripture instructing you to withdraw from him may cause him to view you as the one being disobedient to God's Word.

However, it will require your commitment to the process to continue speaking the truth regardless of his stubborn resistance. Because your mate is the one in authority *(head of the house)*, you must be as certain as one can be that you are in obedience to God. If you are merely spouting out your opinions to resist a prideful stubborn person in authority, you are being foolish and taking unnecessary risks.

Remember, Moses had to endure hard heartedness on both sides of the issue. Pharaoh wasn't the only one uncertain that God sent Moses. The Hebrews assumed God's deliverance would be swift. Their unmet expectations after Moses' initial proclamation to the Pharaoh only served to add more pressure to the situation. Remember, when Pharaoh, filled with pride and anger, told Moses he wouldn't let God's people go and out of spite, demanded that the Hebrew slaves gather their own straw to make bricks? By the same token, your family of origin, children, friends, and church members may misunderstand. Others may applaud your courage to confront your mate with the truth about his behavior – until things appear to get worse. If your mate responds in pride filled anger like Pharaoh you may even find yourself wondering whether or not leaving the unloving, familiar, placating ways of the past is worth it.

When you have days where you find yourself wondering "Lord, what's the use," anchor your hope in God and stand firm.

Remind yourself that the stand you are making is neither obstinate nor arrogant in its demeanor. It is Spirit maintained stamina marked by inner peace while the law of kindness is upon your lips. If you've only been able to tell your mate how you really felt when you were angry, accept that you can learn to tell someone the truth about how you feel without being out of control, insensitive or unkind.

Even when the truth is consistently said in a loving way, your mate still may not accept your comments about how his behavior has been affecting you or that he is being disobedient to God. It may be a while before he is able to see that his irresponsible behavior toward you is having a direct impact upon his relationship with God. But our Heavenly Father, who loves our mates best, knows just how to get His message across. Leave the timing up to Him.

I can't encourage you enough to be as patient with your husband as you want God to be patient with you. Don't try to change your mate. Pray for him. Take care of yourself and your children, if you have any. Change the things *you* need to change about *you*. Can't you feel the courage to jump rising within you?

Could You Be A Jackass?

In Numbers 22 the scripture speaks of a prophet named Balaam and his jackass. The passage records that Balak, the king of Moab, was concerned about the nation of Israel. He described them as "too mighty" for him. He was aware that they had defeated other nations as they traveled on their journey to "the promised land". Now they were setting up camp near Moab. Desperately afraid, he made an attempt to turn the odds in his favor. Having heard that when Balaam blessed folk, they were blessed and when he cursed folk, they were cursed, he sent the elders of Moab to Balaam with "gifts" and a plea to curse the nation of Israel.

Upon delivering Balak's message, Balaam instructed the elders to stay with him overnight while he talked to God about what answer he should give the king. The Bible says that God clearly told Balaam that he couldn't curse the people of Israel because they were blessed and not to go with the elders.

The next morning Balaam informed the elders of God's response. The elders returned and told the king that Balaam would not come with them. Balak, unhappy with the answer, sent more prestigious folk with the message that if Balaam would honor his request, he would promote him and give him great honor. Despite the fact that he told Balak's folks that he couldn't go beyond the Lord's Word, even if Balak gave him his own house filled with silver and gold, he went yet again and asked God could he go and curse Israel.

God told him he could go, but he was instructed to say *only* what God said to him. Greedy for the rewards promised him, Balaam got up the next morning and went with the princes of Moab. His mind was focused on the rewards he was going to collect once he fulfilled his end of the bargain with the king of Moab. Balaam would curse Israel and the king would make sure he got paid.

Initially, Balaam wisely prayed about what he should do. But when God gave him a "no" answer, he should have let that suffice. Instead he asked again so, God decided to "let him have it". *(If God specifically answers "no" to your requests, just trust that He knows best. Don't argue or whine just leave it at that.)*

Balaam was so determined to collect a reward; it didn't matter to him that granting the king's request would require him to disobey God's will for Israel. Disobedience to God always affects more than the person who is disobeying. In this case, it affected the way Balaam treated his jackass.

Sadly, he did not know that on his journey to meet the king, his jackass would see the Angel of the Lord; and the sword he was carrying. Realizing Balaam's life was in danger the jackass moved out of the path of the Angel of the Lord. Upon going in a different direction than Balaam wanted to go, the jackass suffered at the hand of Balaam's anger.

Every time the Angel stood in the path, the animal knew it wasn't safe so she turned in a different direction. Each time, in frustration, Balaam hit the animal with his staff. In one of her attempts to save her master's life, the jackass actually injured him, jamming his foot against a wall, only to be hit again. Finally, afraid of being killed by the Lord's angel if she went forward, or hit again for going backwards, she gave up and fell underneath him.

Completely clueless to what was going on, Balaam prepared to hit her again. The Lord opened the ass' mouth and she said, "What have I done for you to hit me?" Balaam responded, "For making a fool out of me! If I had a sword I'd kill you!" As the conversation continued the jackass said, "Haven't I been loyal to you all my life? All I've ever done is try to help you! Don't you realize that I wouldn't act this way unless there was something seriously wrong?" It wasn't until then that Balaam saw the Angel who told him that his motive for going to see the king of Moab was wrong before the Lord. The Angel also said that if the jackass hadn't turned he would have killed Balaam and left the jackass alive.

Although Balaam quickly apologized and said he'd go back home, the Angel instructed him to go with the princes of Moab and be certain to only speak what God would give him to speak. The scripture then goes on to tell how Balaam blessed the nation of Israel, despite the king's desire to have them cursed.

Though I wouldn't dare call my sisters in Christ jackasses, this scripture has some truth revealing parallels that effectively illustrate aspects of the relationship between a wife and a husband who behaves irresponsibly. As you read the statements below do you see your relationship with your husband?

1. Selfish motives could be affecting your husband's ability to see clearly.
2. Your difficult circumstances may very well be "the Angel of the Lord in the way."
3. As a result of his disobedience to God, your mate may not see the dangers ahead that are obvious to you.
4. Due to impure agenda, your mate may not have a clue as to why you're refusing to do what he wants.
5. Your mate may feel you are making a fool out of him and your loyalty is misplaced.
6. Your attempts to save your husband may cause him injury.
7. Because of the pain of his injury, your mate may lash out at you.
8. In an emotional state of despair, you may simply have "fallen down" underneath your husband.
9. Because you *feel* you're unable to speak the truth about what you see, your mate doesn't understand what's really going on. He is uninformed.
10. The Lord can *open* your mouth and allow you to talk about your pain and concerns with your husband.
11. The Lord will handle your mate's stubbornness.
12. Though satan tried to get your mate to curse you with his lifestyle, God knows how to make sure he blesses you on every hand.

Recognizing that sin hinders a person's heart from *seeing* the truth may help you realize why your husband "just doesn't get it!" He's not dense or stupid. He's just blind and doesn't know it! All he knows is that you aren't staying on the road he's on and you're supposed to be following his lead as you walk your lives together.

You're right. It's not fair that you have to suffer because he can't see. But as his mate, you're connected to each other. What he does will affect you. But it's just as true that what you do will affect him. No matter how much his prideful attitude may suggest otherwise, your patient, firm, loving, courageous stand in God's truth will make an impact.

Sure, you may look disloyal. Yes, as far as he is concerned, you may seem to be a rebellious, stubborn mule. But now you know the truth! You love your husband. You know he has the capacity to love. You wouldn't have married him otherwise. You don't want to see him lose his life with you, the children, or others who care about him — nor does God.

Don't let his lashing out in anger stop you from doing the right thing. You see the dangers ahead! If he's determined to keep going the wrong way, don't help him run head first into God's judgment. Just "fall down" *(Surrender the situation to God. Don't take another step in a direction you **know** it's not safe to go).*

When the Lord gives you the liberty and opportunity, let your mate know that you love him very deeply. Lovingly let him know that you respect him as an adult so much that despite the potentially dangerous consequences, you embrace his freedom to make choices about what he wants and doesn't want in his life. At the same time, your love for him prohibits you from *helping* him do anything that God's Word says will lead to his destruction. Eventually he'll realize that you won't let him coerce you to participate in anything ungodly.

Consequently, you will feel more confident about *surrendering* things to God as you accept and embrace his adulthood.

Dear Father,

Help me to remember my husband is an adult free to make choices — just like me. Like Balak it may take a while for him to see the error of his ways. Please help me to surrender things to You. I recognize that because he is an adult, at times it may be futile to try to "save" him from the consequences of his actions. Help me to never forget that You are there to guide him — and me. Amen.

8. Don't Stop the Reaper's Sickle!

Hebrews 12:10-11 says that God disciplines us for our good that we may share in His holiness. No discipline seems pleasant at the time, but painful. Later on however, it produces a harvest of righteousness and peace for those who have been trained by it.

Since Adam and Eve were given the choice to obey or disobey, all of mankind has a God-given right to make choices for themselves. However, we are not given the right to control the choices made by others. If we habitually prevent others from reaping what they have sown, we are literally hindering their personal growth. Sadly, for many of us, obedience to God's Word is considered only after experiencing the anguish of suffering the consequences of our actions. As human beings, we tend not to grow if we don't suffer. However, as mothers and wives we often prevent our loved ones from benefiting from the discipline of consequence they desperately need. This is called enabling behavior. Have you ever considered how many times you've *helped* your mate to avoid the consequences of his choices, just to save yourself from discomfort? It is painful to see one you love so much suffer the pain and agony of the reaping process, especially if you must suffer with them. Is what we do to *help* really about helping? Or is it more about avoiding?

Jesus told the Pharisees that their traditions made the Word of God of none effect[31]. This led me to ask God, "What traditions do I practice in my life that cause Your Word to be of none effect?" In His love and faithfulness, He showed them to me one after another.

God's Word says that whatever a man sows, that is what he will reap[32]. Have you chosen to reap your mate's consequences for him? When he offends someone, do you try to "fix it" by making excuses for him? When others come to you wounded by your husband's insensitive manner, do you attempt to smooth over breaches he caused in his relationships with others? Or do you lovingly encourage them to take their offense directly to your husband, as instructed in Matthew 18? For many wives these acts have become tradition. Sometimes it works. Lots of times it doesn't. Still other times it makes an even bigger mess of things. The biggest mess is that husbands in this predicament seldom know how people around them really feel. By interfering, we help to perpetuate his lack of understanding and knowledge in dealing with others.

That's just the tip of the iceberg. The undercurrent of our behavior communicates gross disrespect because we attempt to rescue them from life's difficulty. Do the following statements *feel* familiar?

---

[31] Matthew 15:6
[32] Galatians 6:7-8

"It seems clear to me that you do not know what you are doing. You don't seem to be learning from your mistakes. This is much too hard for you to grasp. Step aside. I will rescue the family from your inability to cope with and adapt to life."

We would not dare say anything like that. But can we honestly deny that at times we are very concerned about our husband's ability to *really* handle life? After all, we have seen them repeatedly choose paths that caused our whole family to suffer unnecessarily. If we asked our mates if our behavior has caused them to believe we think of them as incompetent, what would they say? Do we really believe they will *never* learn?

What happened to faith in the wisdom of God? He designed the human brain to process information. The best computer ever created, we are able to analyze and readjust things in our minds in microseconds. Our husbands, creations of the Living God, have that ability. We seem to have forgotten that our Father has promised to lead, guide, provide, and protect His children. That includes our husbands. Sadly, we consistently choose our carnal way of handling difficulty with our mates. Though we see our methods aren't working, we're stuck. We stay on the Merry-Go-Round going round and round, becoming more and more nauseated. Every time we try to fix breaches in *his* relationships or make excuses for his failure to follow through on his word, we are protecting and controlling him like we would a toddling child.

Furthermore, it is a feeble attempt to control the flow of pain coming our way. Unfortunately for him, what starts out looking like moral support ends up feeling like you're trying to control his life. My husband once told me I was controlling. All I could think at the time was, "Well, isn't that the pot calling the kettle black?!" To my embarrassment his assessment was accurate. What an eye opener to discover that my attempts to influence my husband to do the *right* thing caused him to "feel controlled." The fact was ***I had been trying to control aspects of the relationship outside my ability to control.*** I needed to practice the familiar Prayer of Serenity by Saint Francis of Assisi.

"Dear God, grant me the serenity to accept the things I cannot change; the courage to change the things I can and the wisdom to know the difference."

A sincere request for a life of serenity *(peace and calm)* begins by asking for the ability to accept *(embrace)* that there are things we cannot change. At the heart of a controlling nature is the demand that things change to suit us. In I Corinthians 13, God's Word lists the attributes of one who loves. Recorded there is that love does not demand its own way. Having made up our minds to turn away from the wickedness of an unloving and demanding spirit, you may find accepting the things you cannot change a challenging task. When a husband's behavior does not reinforce his wife's sense of worth in the marital relationship, her demand that he love her is a sure fire way to keep the Merry-Go-Round going.

Meditate for a moment on the reality that even though you are jumping off the Merry-Go-Round, at the same time you must accept your husband *as he is*. At this point your heart may be screaming, "ACCEPT WHAT!! You've got to be kidding!! There is no way I'm going to keep putting up with that foolishness! I've had enough!" Some may feel like ripping this page right out of the book. Your emotions may have taken over so much that you might have missed the finer point of what I said. I didn't say accept your husband's behavior. I said accept *him*. There is a vast difference.

Ephesians 1:6 tells us that we are "accepted in the Beloved." If your mate is a Christian, God has accepted him. If that's true and it is, then who are you to reject him? Rejecting our mates is not the answer. However, it is acceptable to reject our mate's harmful behavior. It is important that we keep the difference in meaning between those two statements crystal clear. Even if your mate is not a Christian, making the distinction between him and his behavior will make a positive impact.

Too often we have sought to reject our mates irresponsible behavior only to leave him feeling that *he* is unacceptable. *He* has been rejected. His response, reject her back. Her response, reject him still more. Round and round we go *(I'm getting nauseous again.)* Acceptance of the person is a major component of agape love because it wisely distinguishes between embracing the person and not their acts. Remember how Jesus accepted the woman violently thrown before him after having been caught in the very act of adultery? What about His acceptance of Peter even after he had denied Him three times? We must seek the Holy Spirit regarding how to balance accepting those He loves with rejecting sinful behavior.

God has given each individual the right to choose whether or not they will love *(obey)* Him. He does <u>not</u> demand that we love Him. *He does* make efforts to *cause us to be aware* of the reality *of His love for us* and then gives us the freedom to respond or not respond, in obedience. Whether one chooses to respond in faith-filled, love motivated obedience, or self-centered, shortsighted, doubt inspired dis-obedience, the Word of God assures us that we will all have our turn before the judgment seat of Christ to receive whatever we have coming. What we receive will be up to each person to choose. Take a moment to prayerfully consider if you have been attempting to decide what your mate chooses. The fact of the matter is, you can only decide what *you* want to receive.

Dear Father,

I wasn't seeing clearly how much my behavior was exhibiting a lack of trust and confidence in You. You started the work in my husband's life.

Your Word promises that You will finish it. My heart has been so filled with doubt. You gave my husband the right to choose life or death. I have tried to MAKE him choose life as I see it. I even tried to be his savior by rescuing him from the consequences of his actions when You may have wanted to use those consequences as a catalyst to draw him closer to You. I was wrong.

*I need You to show me how to do what Your Word tells **me** to do. Help me to be balanced in my thinking. I know that no matter how insurmountable things may look, nothing is too hard for You. Help me to stay connected to trustworthy, wise Christian people who will affirm my faith in You, while giving me the love and support I will need as I refuse to repeat the lies of the past. Amen.*

9. Reality [✓] Anger: Yours & His

"I've had all I can stand and I can't stand no more!"

Popeye's statement of limitation still rings true in the hearts of those who feel bullied by the Brutus' of life. We think, "How wonderful it could be if we could simply eat spinach and pulverize the ones we feel are not doing right by us." We ask, "What happened to the guy that charmed my sox off? Where is the man who said he *loved* me so much he'd do anything to see me smile? Who is this unambitious, out of touch, lackadaisical...? *(You get the picture. I better stop now before you get upset.)* **Surely** this guy who gets in my bed wanting sex isn't him!"

When expressing a desire to talk with our husbands about their lack of response to our needs, we are often thwarted by their tendency to disregard how important issues of safety and provision are to us. This is a vicious cycle where the wife believes she is pursuing solutions and the husband is avoiding any type of confrontation or denies the problem altogether. Who wouldn't be angry after going through this for months, years, or dare I say decades?

For some of us our husband's irresponsibility has reached a level we will no longer tolerate. We don't want a divorce. We want to smash him to smithereens. Oh, but wait! *Real* Christians don't feel like that, do they? You better believe they do.

My best friend talked about how glad she was that Jesus was in her life to keep things in check. Otherwise she would have been calling me to tell me her husband's body parts were all over the house. I personally recall moments when I was so angry inside that I literally put my knees in my chest and held my legs together to fight off the incredible urge to take my feet and shove my husband out of our bed. The frustration of it all overwhelmed me. We couldn't seem to keep anything. We were consistently behind in our bills. Loss and lack was everywhere and as far as I was concerned, it was entirely *his* fault. I felt rejected, unwanted, unloved, and justified in allowing my anger to explode. Out of control, I would yell and stomp attempting to make him see how bad things were. At times I even swore and threw things around but that didn't help. *(Do you act like this?)* In the end I had to face reality. My anger was helping satan destroy my marriage and me.

The loss of homes, cars, jobs, and relationships with others, to name a few, are legitimate reasons to be angry.

Worst of all is the loss of our own sense of self-respect and dignity. Our sin nature feels entitled to whatever action we deem appropriate. After all, who wants to see their children wearing worn out and out grown clothing, or shoes? Who wants to live with no utilities, unreliable cars, bill collectors calling, or bankruptcy? Who wants to admit that they contribute to the frustration, discouragement, emotional abuse, and provocation of their children? Nobody.

Ironically, our husbands' failure to act and our desire to please God in our relationships often distorts the appearance of our anger so that it is not easily identified. Some of us take the anger we feel toward our husband and aim it inward at ourselves. The guilt of a failing relationship makes our hearts heavy with grief. Sadness is spreading its gloomy presence into places it does not belong. The joy of our salvation is being sapped of its energy like a rose in the desert sun. Our bodies are filled with tension. Our health is being affected.

We want to let our mates know how we feel but confrontation is not our way so we begin to exhibit what is called passive-aggressive manipulation. He asks us to do something. We never get it done. He wants sex. We don't. When he isn't making the basic needs of our family a priority, we *forget* to do things that are important to him. We think, "why should he be the only one to get what he wants? There are two people in this relationship." *(Can you feel the speed of the Merry-Go-Round picking up?)* After a while it seems that emotionally disconnecting ourselves from the marriage is the only choice.

Others of us have projected the anger onto our children contributing to the gradual demise of their fragile sense of worth and confidence. If we don't get a handle on it, chances are they will make the same mistakes. Still others of us have no problem displaying our anger. We say the first thing that comes to our mind. All we want is him to stop being a wimp and be responsible, like a man. Unfortunately, we have the effectiveness of a hand grenade that is used to start a car. Only a spark is needed, not a blast. No matter what negative form our anger takes it gives our mate the justification he needs to withdraw further from relationship. Their further withdrawal leaves us feeling more rejected, more unloved, and angrier. Someone has to change for this Merry-Go-Round to stop.

At first it is difficult to reconcile how *our* changing is going to improve circumstances if our husbands refuse to cooperate. In our opinion we have already changed quite a bit. Many of us have already made numerous attempts to change *things.* We feel very strongly that before we do anything else, it is our husband's turn to do some changing. Our hidden agenda is, "Keep the focus off me and on my husband. He's the head of the house, isn't he? He is the one ultimately responsible for all this, isn't he? So why doesn't he _do_ something?"

Amazingly, his lack of motivation is not the issue. The truth of the matter is his anger is *his* problem. Your anger is *your* problem. The issue now is what are you going to do with *your* anger? Pray? Certainly. But that is not all. You will let your husband know you are angry in new, more honest and healthy ways. As an adult, you are free to choose your actions. As a Christian, the wisdom and grace of God is available to help you assist your mate in understanding your personal limitations. For example, when he asks things of you that you don't want to do, be honest. Simply tell him "no" at the beginning. For example, "Honey, right now I am so angry with you that I don't want to do anything for you." When he asks why you won't do things, kindly, calmly, and honestly tell him. At times you may need to say, "I love you honey, but because of ..., I don't trust you to handle my affairs anymore."

Like anything else new you learn, you may feel uneasy at first. It may help to practice what and how you will say things with a close friend. Don't start with something that is a large issue between you. Start with something that seems trivial or insignificant. When you feel confident enough begin to address issues more close to your heart. Although you will be nervous and your insides may even be shaking, do it anyway. As you continue to spend time with the Lord, He will show you things you can do to express your anger in a more healthy way. Later you will be amazed at how much less tension you feel in your body. In time you will find confidence increasing to the extent that you are more comfortable being who you are, instead of who others want you to be. In your husband's eyes, you may appear to be the doomsayer who always poured rain on his parades; he may even see you as disloyal when you share your situation with others. Oh yes, your husband will resist, but if he truly loves you, he will gradually accept *you*.

For some the thought of doing such things is frightening. *You* are paralyzed with fear because of his anger. The way you respond to that fear is something else *you* can change. Are you afraid you are in physical danger? If so, read on.

Dealing with the Fear of Hubby's Anger

One of the most fearful experiences a neglected wife can encounter is the anticipation of her husband's rage. The dread of painful distancing, intimidation, and rejection tactics husbands may frequently use, often cause wives to live below their God-ordained privilege.

For me this dilemma created an awareness of a huge gulf between the woman I really was and the one I portrayed. Extreme insecurity robbed me. It was so much easier to blame my husband. When others asked me "If you believe what he's asking you to do is wrong, why don't you simply tell him no," the only honest answer I could come up with was, "Because, he might get mad." Why wasn't I worried about God's displeasure at sinful disobedience?

Rarely do wives realize that they are more concerned about displeasing their husbands than they are about displeasing God. The truth is they are really afraid to confront their husbands with their true feelings because his anger is almost always coupled with rejection. Frankly, we already feel that his lack of interest proves we're unlovable.

Irresponsible folk who are no longer "getting their way" tend to resist changes in the relationship by attempting some form of retaliation. For many, their husband's emotional retaliation seems like death itself. Though it gives no guarantees, courage is vital to your emotional well being. As may be his pattern, a displeased irresponsible man may selfishly use his anger to maintain the familiarity of the Merry-Go-Round.

The reality of verbal, emotional, or even physical abuse can petrify a woman struggling to get control of her life. It is in moments of stabbing anxiety that we must surrender our fears to the Lord. If your husband tends to be physically violent when he is angry, you will need the help of others in the Body of Christ even more as you go through this process. Ask God to give you someone (friend, family member, counselor, support group, etc.) who can encourage and build you up. The fear experienced by women married to irresponsible men can in time, be overcome by genuine trust in God. Take courage. There is hope.

NOTE:
Because a man's anger can become extremely volatile and terribly frightening I must urge you to seek a safe place for yourself and the children if your physical safety is an issue. Trying to stay in the home in these cases is

not only emotionally and mentally damaging; it can be deadly. You need to do more than pray.

Protecting your mate from the consequences of his actions is not in the best interest of you, your children, or your mate. Please remember that domestic violence not only displeases God, it is against the law. Many states have begun to implement laws that are much more effective than in times past.

Ask the Holy Spirit for courage to call your local church or crisis hot line for safe havens in your area. Don't wait for you or your children to be maimed or killed. Get help!

Vashti's Syndrome

Anger that is physically intimidating or violent isn't the only reason women have followed their husbands into the sin of irresponsibility. Awareness of his wife's fear of being abandoned makes for many a manipulative statement. Fear of abandonment runs deep in many women. That fear is not outside of reason. Women's anxiety about abandonment is fed by the divorce statistics, which reveal men's tendency to treat their marriages like they are disposable diapers. The scripture even records such a case in point. As we read Esther chapter one we learn about the plight of Vashti. This woman suffered something wives have dreaded for centuries – exile from relationship. Her husband, King Ahasuerus, prepared a feast for all the nobles of the Persian Empire. This feast was so grand that he instructed his servants to "give every man his desire." This indulgence went on for 180 days. On the seventh day the king in typical male style began bragging about the beauty of his wife. To prove his point he sent his servants after her with instructions for her to return "in the crown royal" so his drunken noble guests could gaze at her.

To his dismay, Vashti refused to come. Scripture does not record her reasoning but most wives would agree that to display your beauty before a group of men you know have been drinking and indulging themselves for seven days, is not a safe place for a beautiful female. When she stood up for herself, against the foolish request of her husband, in anger he exiled and eventually replaced her.

Often as ministers have taught from this text, the focus is placed on how a wife takes a risk when she does not do as her husband asks. Therefore she should *obey* her husband. Very few have given attention to the reality that it is unreasonable to expect a wife to *display* herself before a bunch of drunken men.

Unfortunately, Vashti's plight is a harsh reality. When wives' responses cause their husbands great disappointment, many husbands abandon the marriage and replace their wives with someone else they believe will be more accommodating. It is this sad fact that is at the heart of many a wife's choice to enable their husband's sinful behavior. What if he is displeased to the point where he divorces me? What if he decides that he will have an affair behind my back? The "what-ifs" produce a Merry-Go-Round within a Merry-Go-Round.

Nevertheless, earlier in chapter 2, the section on His Contribution, I mentioned the need for wives to maintain personal integrity when their husbands compromise. I cannot emphasize enough how vital is that you *keep your life chaste*.

Do not allow yourself to be deceived. Following your husband's lead when he is being disobedient to the Lord will **not** be acceptable to God. It is written that we ought to obey God rather than man.[33] A believer's first responsibility is to

---
[33] Acts 5:29

love God and as a result of that love, obey His Word. When obeying the scripture we must make certain we are looking at God's Word in context. To say that a woman is obeying God's Word by appeasing her husband, when he is committing obvious sin, is to take God's command completely out of context. Though He says, "a wife is concerned about how to please her husband," He has also said that if your husband does not "obey *the* word" you may be able to "win him" by your "conversation"[34] or manner of living. That manner of living is clearly described as being chaste.

The Greek word interpreted chaste from I Peter 3:4 is the word *hagnos* which means innocent, clean, and pure. I am sure you agree that there is nothing chaste about lying. Earlier *(Chapter 2: His Contribution)* I mentioned briefly how the Holy Spirit can use a wife's innocent, clean, and pure behavior to create the kind of contrast that will draw attention to areas where her husband's integrity is lacking. The wife's implementation of responsible patterns in areas where she makes decisions is where the actual "jump from the Merry-Go-Round" takes place.

Up to now your attempts to *please* your husband may have caused you to compromise your integrity. The choice to please your mate at any cost helps keep the Merry-Go-Round spinning. Be determined to become a woman of consistent integrity. I cannot emphasize enough the importance of no longer allowing the poor stewardship of your husband to be yours.

At times our desire to either please our husbands or avoid their fury can short-circuit our convictions. It is simply foolish to compromise God's Word for any relationship, even one you vowed to maintain a lifetime. Frankly, a lifetime is a drop in the bucket when compared to eternity. Think long and hard. Would you rather be exiled from a marriage that

---

[34] I Peter 3:1-7

can at best only last a lifetime, or would you have God exile you from His presence for eternity?

If blissful eternity with God is too far away to be of adequate motivation, consider this. Wives who signed joint tax returns were prosecuted for tax evasion, *along with* their husbands. Because their signature was on the joint return, it mattered not to the judge that they did not have a clue about what their husbands earned, or that they weren't aware their husband's had illegally dodged taxes to obtain a large refund. Not only is it unwise, it is poor stewardship to stay in the dark about your family resources. Learn what you need to. Be informed.

That's not all. Laws that once prohibited a wife from testifying against her husband no longer provide the same level of protection from prosecution. Women who permit their husbands to abuse their children are being prosecuted for neglect and abuse, *along with* their husbands. As sad as it is that women fail to respond because they are afraid, it has not stopped many of them from spending unnecessary time behind bars.

If you are afraid to stand up to your husband because he may leave you, prepare yourself for inner and outer struggle. As frightening as it may seem, place your husband on the altar of sacrifice. *(NO!! I don't mean kill him. I mean turn your concerns over to the Lord.)* Ask the Lord to grant you courage to stand firm in your convictions. This does not mean that you have to be obstinate. It simply means that you will not be unwise and succumb to intimidating tactics. Choose instead to trust God with the outcome.

Heretofore you may have fumed over how much you are expected to "be a saint" while your mate stubbornly acts like he ain't. The unmet yearnings in your soul may cause you to wonder, "When is it going to be *my* turn!" Pain and loss also shout their cries for relief, at any cost. But, don't let any of those things deter you. Don't back down. Don't give in. Stand firm in the conviction of your faith in God. After you have done all you know to do in your standing, continue, despite how bad things look, to stand in the righteousness of your faith in Christ. Understand that you are not to *act* like a virtuous woman. You need to *be* a virtuous woman.

Dear Father,

Help me to stand firm! Make me to understand that I will always have You. Don't let fear of being alone or losing my relationship with my mate keep me from doing what pleases You. Amen.

10. Will the "Real" Virtuous Woman, Please Stand Up?

The "virtuous woman" of Proverbs 31 has been everything from a goal to an impossible dream in the minds of women who love God for millennia. This woman gets up early, serves those who serve her, conducts business, and maintains an impeccable reputation. She is described as a very productive and gracious woman who impacts the lives of those she encounters. In fact, she is so wise in her dealings that even her husband's colleagues took note of how blessed he was to have her for a wife. To top it off despite how busy she is she speaks kindly to everyone.

Incredible! In our age of information technology it's easy to see this woman was ahead of her time. She knew what *time management* was before the phrase was ever coined. She exemplified balance in her relationships with those she served, as well as those who served her. She is recorded as handling her responsibilities, gifts, and talents so well that she was able to purchase property on her own at a time when women were considered unsuited for such things. *Thank God that era is over.*

For many of us gloominess hangs over our heads when reading this Biblical passage. Because she sounds like Wonder Woman, we feel we won't ever measure up. We tell ourselves, "There's no way in the world that I can do all that. I can barely keep up with the stuff I have to do now. I give up." But don't give up. Listen to this.

There is a Hebrew word translated virtue in this verse of scripture called *chayil*. Every other time it is used in scripture, it is used to speak of strength, courage, valor, and wealth. The King James translators were very accurate in choosing the word *virtue.* In the 1600's when King James commissioned Bible scholars to translate the original Bible cannon into English, the word virtue meant, manly courage, valor. *(See the obsolete notation in your dictionary.)*

Men and women of that day understood that Proverbs 31 was speaking of a woman who was so filled with courage that she was able to go into a "man's world" and run her home and her own business. In a time when little girls grew up regularly seeing females silenced as if their thoughts could not possibly contribute anything worthwhile, the scripture's account of how the elders of the community respected this woman of virtue is impressive.

Women married to men who behave irresponsibly can learn something from this woman. It is possible to have the respect of men instead of being seen as an object for their folly or a slave. But you won't have anyone's respect if your behavior habitually reflects cowardice. Standing up to your loved one's anger and resistance against the changes you are making in your life will take consistent determination and valor. Refuse to bow to frequent feelings of anxiety and fear. Be who you really are versus who others want you to be. Rely heavily on the leading of the Holy Spirit. He knows what virtue in your life will look like.

When fear of divorce or abuse come upon you, standing up for yourself and your children may seem like risking your lives. In some cases it won't be the appearance of risk. You will in fact be risking your life and the lives of your children. Choosing to no longer enable the irresponsible behavior of your husband definitely provides "threatening conditions." To women courageous enough to change enabling behaviors of the past, it will feel like death is all around.

But when the Holy Spirit balances a genuine confidence in God on the inside with an outward manifestation of courage, this confidence yields the fruit of God's Spirit - real peace. Your heart can become so filled with calm that it brings emotional stability amidst frightening conditions. You will be empowered to exemplify kindness as you patiently wait for God to accomplish His purpose in the lives of you and your mate. It is in the absence of hysterics and other types of emotional "drama" that the root causes for habitually unpaid bills, marital and parental neglect, etc. can be identified and addressed more readily.

One of the places the Hebrew word *chayil* is used in scripture speaks of men who risked their lives to bring King David a drink of water. When the king saw how great a risk they took on his behalf, he was overwhelmed. He could not bring himself to drink the water. Instead, counting himself unworthy of such an honor, he poured it out as an offering before the Lord. These men of valor refused to let fear or life-threatening conditions dictate how they would respond to the need of their beloved king.

As virtuous women, we are challenged to hold our responses up to the light of God's Word to reveal confidence in our Savior, or cowardice. The possible death of your relationship with your husband and maybe your relationships with members of your church up to now may have been painful and frightening enough to prevent you from taking non-traditional, yet biblical action *(Merry-Go-Round jumping)*. But now you know the truth about manipulation, pacifying, and indifference. You know you must jump from the madness, by faith.

Like King David, your beloved husband is in need of a drink of the water of life in Christ. Are you willing to risk the life of your ineffective coping skills? Can God use your responses to provide your husband with a satisfying drink of Christ's life? Is there a desire stirring within you to overcome your fear?

If you have decided to respond courageously, my prayer is that your husband be overwhelmed by your demonstration of love, count himself unworthy of such honor, and respond by pouring himself out to the Lord by loving you as the scripture teaches.

Are You Sarah's Daughter?

I Peter 3:6 says that if wives "do well and are not afraid with any amazement" they are the *daughters of Sarah*. The reality that Sarah was a woman of faith is often understated. The book of Genesis tells us that the faith of Abram *[Exalted Father]* and Sarai *[Dominative]* caused God to give them the new names of Abraham *[Father of Many Nations]* and Sarah *[Princess]*. Their old names no longer described who they were. The courage Abram exhibited at times seems to overshadow the fact that when Abram left all the familiarity of home and family, so did Sarai. Abram's God challenged his faith and devotion as if to say, "How much do you really believe in Me?" As true as it is that women of that day were commonly viewed as little more than property, it does not eliminate the truth that Sarai's faith was also challenged.

Imagine the anguish Sarai must've felt. You've been married to Abram for many years. He loves you and you love him. You are aware of the longing he has for a son, yet year after year, nothing. One day he tells you about a conversation he's had with his God. He has been instructed to take the entire family, servants, flocks, and all to some unknown destination[35].

Initially, fear of the unknown wreaks havoc on your sense of security. But you love your husband. There is no question that you are going with him. Besides, when he speaks of Yahweh *[Hebrew name for Jehovah God]* something in your heart knows that his God – is God. There is no doubt in your mind that as long as you have Abram and Yahweh everything will work out. Your fear gives way to a sense of adventure derived from the confidence you have in Yahweh. After all, He has prospered you and your husband thus far.

Days turn into weeks, weeks into months, and months into years. Still no baby. Every year you rejoice with your servants as their families grow around you. The love you have to give a child you pour into theirs. But nothing satisfies the ache in your heart at not being able to give your husband a son. Everyone comments on your natural beauty, but it does not replace your desire to be a beautiful mother.

To make matters worse, during your journey your husband becomes so afraid pagans are going to kill him because you are so beautiful that he permits you to be taken

---

[35] Genesis 12:1

for some other man's harem[36]. Experiencing betrayal is a blow to any woman's sense of security. It could be that Sarai struggled with thoughts about her barrenness being the "true" reason for Abram's willingness to give her away. Unable to reconcile God's promise with his actions, she may have thought, "Why would a childless man who believes God told him he would be the father of many nations be so afraid for his life that he'd lie and permit some other man to take his wife?" It's plain and simple; fear paralyzes faith.

Many women of our culture cannot empathize with a woman who desperately wants a child but cannot conceive. In that time, barrenness was considered a curse. To have life growing within you was a blessing, especially if it was male. If you couldn't give your husband a child, you were considered worthless. Despite God's promise that their child would come *through her*, Sarai made a choice to give her husband to another woman. This was just as foolish as Abram's giving her to pagans.

Though the book of Genesis does not give a detailed account of all Sarai's responses to being barren, betrayed, and sharing her husband, the mention of her name in Hebrews 11:11 confirms that she had her own faith in God. Whether God's conversation with the pagans Abram turned her over to was the answer to Sarai's prayers, we don't know for certain. But we do know that before all things were said and done, *her faith* pleased God.

Like Abram and Sarai, you and your husband may have made foolish choices. However, you must not forget that also like Abram and Sarai, God can change your character so much that it's like changing your name. He can turn your weeping into rejoicing and your mourning into joy. Proverbs 6:20 instructs us to forsake not our mother's law. If we are Sarah's daughters, we will demonstrate the courage she had

---

[36] Genesis 12:11-20

as we go through times when we feel betrayed by our husbands.

Dear Father,

Help me to build my hope on Christ, the One who started and will give me what I need to finish my faith. As I trust that You will do what Your word says, I believe my emotions will be anchored to an indestructible foundation. That foundation will see me through this life, its trials, joys and tribulations, into eternity – just like Mother Sarah. Amen.

11. Just How Do You Show Respect to an Irresponsible Mate?

Now that you realize that you have made some contributions to the way things are, and that you've got to work on getting the log(s) out of your own eye first, and muster up the courage to put some works with the faith you profess to have in God, you're probably wondering, "Christina, just how am I going to show respect to my irresponsible mate?" I'm glad you asked that question. Paul said in Romans 7:18 that he couldn't find *how* to perform that which was good. Oh my how I could identify with that! At times we find that no matter how much we want to do something that pleases God, we just can't seem to figure things out. When it comes to trying to respect our mates, too many of us are hindered by memories of the times when our mates abused their authority. Too many of us recall numerous times when we allowed ourselves to feel banished to the land of miserable silence when we tried to express our concerns, because we thought that was what God wanted.

Well ladies, banish those thoughts! That's definitely not what God has in mind. To believe that He gets pleasure from your misery is to forget everything the Bible teaches about Him. I won't get into that now because that's another Merry-Go-Round all together.

You've come this far because you want to be obedient to God's word. That is a great beginning. Now we need to go further in the process. If you intend to respect your husband, who is behaving irresponsibly, you need to recognize that the way you will respect him looks slightly different from the way you'd respect one who is consistently responsible.

Often we spin our wheels trying to understand things because, quite plainly, our prideful sin nature causes us to struggle with acknowledging that we cannot understand *every*thing. When it comes to God's Word there are times when we must simply obey regardless of whether or not we understand. This is one of those times.

The key to respecting an irresponsible man rests in some truths that we must simply accept. Take a few days and meditate on the following three truths. Embrace them. They will under gird your efforts with the substance true respect is made of.

- **Contrary to popular belief, respect does NOT have to be earned.** As Christians, we must remember that mankind is created in the image of God. When we cannot find behavior worthy of respect in our mates, we must be respectful based on the reality that of all the life forms God created, mankind is the only one in which God chose to imbed His image. This alone makes ALL humanity worthy of respect. I know that this is the exact opposite of what we are familiar with, but Colossians 4:6 challenges us to *let our conversation always be full of grace and seasoned with salt*. Since grace is favor that we receive even though we don't deserve it, this scripture is implying that how we treat others is not to be based on what we feel they deserve; especially since all of us have come short of God's glory. This means that the only thing any of us deserves is death, hell, and the grave. Too often we feel comfortable devaluing our mates because of their irresponsible behavior. Just like a $100 does not decrease in value because it has been handled by people with dirty hands and then stepped on, likewise our mate's value before God is not lessened because of their irresponsibility. And since we know that salt contains properties that *preserve, enhance, and melt* we are challenged by this scriptural instruction to make certain that our conversation and behavior does all it can to preserve the relationship without the ungodly tools of manipulation and pacification, enhance the relationship by choosing to only speak those things that edify (see Ephesians 4:29), all the while softening their hearts by the consistent expression of the Fruit of the Spirit; especially gentleness and kindness. Because doing these things will cause us to increase in maturity as we walk with God, asking our Heavenly Father to empower us to embrace these truths as we obey His Word is a must.

- **For a while it will look like you are being disrespectful when in fact it will be the opposite.** So often we appease our mates in an attempt to express love. Unfortunately, while our behavior on the surface says, "See honey, I'm here for you," in the undercurrent the *man/warrior* we long to see in our mates has no challenge to rise to. Galatians 6:4 instructs us to *let every man prove his own work*. Too often we are doing that work for them because, as I said earlier, on some level we do not believe that our mates are capable adults. As wives reach a place where we recognize that God has given our mates the ability to choose who they desire to be, we can minister to the part of our husbands' heart that has longed for someone to believe in them. When we don't believe in their capability, it is emasculating. Consider examples mentioned earlier (i.e. your mate has asked you to speak to the children about something they are upset about. Maybe you have made calls to smooth things over with family members he has offended). If you are like many wives, you have allowed yourself to become the middle man. Think about the following analogy. Your becoming the middle man is just as ridiculous as helping an able bodied adult across the street. In fact, when you see a healthy adult crossing the street you make no attempt to assist them because the thought simply doesn't enter your mind. I remember when I decided that I would no longer be the middleman for my teenage children or my husband. Every time my husband or one of my children began to file a complaint for me to give to a third party I responded with the question, "Have you talked to them?" If they had not, I reminded them of Matthew 18:15. After all, if they could communicate their concerns to me that was more than enough proof that they were capable of communicating with the person with whom they were having a problem. Boy was it uncomfortable! My husband and children were angry with me for several months. There were many times when I was tempted to throw in the towel. But the Lord gave me the resolve I needed to hang in there. In less than a year, their relationships changed. There were times when it wasn't pretty or comfortable to be at home. But I kept assuring them that they could do it. On the surface they felt like I had – angry and frustrated. But as time passed in the undercurrent they came to believe that I refused to speak for them because I had confidence in their God given ability to communicate the concerns of their own heart. More than that, I had confidence in God's desire to help His children mature. Even if He chose to do it through the refining properties of sadness (Ecclesiastes 7:3).

- **God is more committed to getting you and your mate through the process than you are.** Romans 8:28 is more than a memory verse. It is a reality. If you love God and you are reading this book in response to His call to your heart regarding respecting your husband, He is going to work *every* thing out for your good. You have wisely chosen to follow and obey Him. He is going to complete the work that He started in you. Believe Him!

As you embrace the above truths, you may now be wondering what specific things you can do to show your husband respect. There's no way I can give you a list of every possible way to respect your husband. Since the Holy Spirit is the true Guide, He will be the One to give you expressions of respect that are tailor made for your husband. But here's a short list of ten things you can do, just to point you in the right direction.

1. **Pray FOR your husband and ABOUT the situation.** Too often we go to God to complain about our mates, instead of really praying for him. Be encouraged to

pray *about* the situation you're in - and *for* your husband. The truth is God knows everyone better than they know themselves. Don't forget to give God a chance to talk with you. Besides, you're going to need His help to follow through on the rest of this list. In fact, who better to go to with problems we're having with someone else?

2. **Accept and rejoice in your mate's individuality - and yours.** While your mate may be irresponsible, they are also created in the image of God, and therefore, they are capable of choosing their own path. Even though you long for the "two to become one," remember that when the two of you stand before God, it will be as individuals. Your mate won't be able to pull an "Adam" and blame you for anything. He will have to answer to God for his own choices, as will the rest of us. Stay focused on what you want God to say to you when it's your turn to give an account for the things you've done!

3. **Accept them - reject their behavior.** Don't allow yourself to see your mate's irresponsible behavior and their person as one. Remember, their behavior isn't all there is to them. After all, there had to be some positive things about them, or you wouldn't have gotten involved with them. Right?

4. **Accept the reality that they CAN do better.** Since your mate may be consistently making irresponsible choices, you may have come to believe that he is hopeless. Don't believe that! Jesus came so that even the vilest of sinners could be empowered to change. To believe there is no hope is simply failing to trust God. Don't ever forget that by the power of the Holy Spirit, anyone willing to accept Christ and apply God's Word to his (or her) life can be changed.

5. **Be kind as often as you can do it - genuinely.** Accept the fact that irresponsibility does not make them unworthy of receiving kindness. No one likes being spoken to or treated harshly, no matter what they've done. Remember that kindness is a fruit of God's Spirit.[37] Express it!
6. **Be patient!** Give your mate room to make mistakes and learn from them. When a person has been irresponsible for a long time, it takes a while for them to become accustomed to handling their affairs responsibly. Besides, you need patience anyway, so you can be mature and complete, lacking nothing in Christ. This is the perfect opportunity to develop it!
7. **Don't lie to them about how their behavior affects you and the way you feel about them.** As honestly and as lovingly as possible, make them aware of any personal limits you may have with your current circumstances. Let your yea be yea and your nay be nay. Don't be fickle.
8. **Don't do what is their responsibility to do.** (i.e., when they don't pay the bill collectors as they promised - don't make or receive the call explaining why the payment wasn't made.) If you are used to "screening" calls, making excuses, and the like, stop. Adults can speak for themselves. Treat them as a capable adult.
9. **Don't try to control them or their choices - anymore.** You may have been trying to stop any consequences for their behavior from affecting you. They may have experienced these actions as your trying to control them. If God leads you to apologize for your controlling behavior - do it!

---

[37] Galatians 5:22

10. Don't be a hypocrite! Maintain integrity by being responsible when you make choices. Otherwise, you're just the pot calling the kettle black.

As you begin to apply these practices to your life, there is no doubt that you will see how desperately you need God! It is difficult to honor and respect someone who is dishonoring and disrespecting you. But don't sweat it! It is not impossible! What seems impossible to mankind is a tap dance for God! You've got His Spirit dwelling within you! It is His desire to empower you to obey His word. Even though it may not understand it, you've got everything you need to get this job done.

Dear Father, thank you for giving me some additional clarity on what I can do to respect my husband. Somehow things have seemed so impossible. But I know that what is impossible with man is possible with You. Help me to place my confidence in Your ability and not in what I perceive to be my mate's inability. Help me to accept what I need to accept and do what I need to do not based on how I feel, but on my desire to please and love You. I yield myself to Your will in this marriage. I really do believe that you will empower me to get this job done! Amen.

12. A Word for Wise Men: What to do When Your Wife is a Pain!

Have you ever experienced a relationship with a loving sister? If not, imagine you have a sister. She loves you. You love her. Though there is the typical sibling bickering between you, there is no doubt in your mind that when she gives you advice about women it is with your and the family's best interest at heart. I am your sister in Christ. We have the same Father. We have been taught by our Father to help each other. It is my sincere desire to help.

As you read this chapter of my book, I pray it becomes obvious that you have a loving sister in me. I realize it may be difficult to hear some of the things I will say, but rest assured that I share these things with the best interest of the family at heart. Like a sister born to you I will be honest and maybe just as annoying. But after all is said *(or in this case written)* and done, you will know that the values our Father passed down to us have been preserved and are available to you.

I believe you are a man who has asked God for help. You are no longer in denial about the destructiveness of your passive tendencies toward lack of involvement and irresponsibility. You believe it is important to understand what's been going on in order to begin truly loving your wife. You have a genuine desire to flee the irresponsible patterns of the past.

You may have read Ephesians 5:25-33 where the apostle Paul wrote that a husband ought to love his wife...

- As Christ loves the church.

- As his own body.

- As himself.

The first and third instructions are simple but they often become complicated by personal perceptions. Some have said, "Christ was God in the flesh. He was able to love in ways that I have yet to comprehend. I'm only human." Others have said, "If a man doesn't love himself, he can't love his wife. He must first love himself."

Consequently, these perceptions have many men stuck. Others are smug when using the excuse "I don't know what to do." Hence the question, "How can I love to my wife if I don't know specifically what to do?" It is the Lord's instruction to love your wife, *as your own body*, that is most effective in clarifying what action should be taken. So try treating your wife like she's a *real* pain in the neck. ☺

Responses in times of physical pain are clear, precise, and at times automatic. If a husband were to view his troubled marriage as he would his body when in a physical crisis, his understanding of what his responses should be would become much less clouded.

For example, there are times when a person goes to do something, and due to the neglect of his body, the muscles required to perform the task are unable to respond. This inability immediately sends a message to the brain. "I can't! You haven't taken care of me! My ability to do this task is nada, zip, zilch!" In other words, the man experiences *pain*. Suddenly, without much forethought, the task originally attempted comes to an abrupt halt.

Many times, the painful place will be automatically favored. If the pain is in the back, the injured person may sit or lie down in order to "rest." Later, they may begin to lessen the amount of pressure put upon it. The person no longer attempts to move heavy objects without the aid of others.

Sometimes, if tasks must be done in order to provide for themselves and their family, therapy or training on how to accomplish tasks without risking further damage may be obtained. Forcing a bad back to continue taking on burdens despite its weakened state inevitably sustains more damage. The potential for permanent damage to delicate tissue is too great to risk forcing oneself to lift heavy objects. Therefore, it is decided that no heavy lifting will ever be done again, period. Horrible yet avoidable damage can occur when the body is frequently called upon to do tasks that it is not prepared or conditioned to do. No one in their right mind would force a damaged muscle to perform the tasks a healthy, well-conditioned muscle could undertake because the pain would be unbearable. Would a healthy, rational person welcome an opportunity to become debilitated? Absolutely not!

In the absence of a healthy diet and regular exercise, when the brain sends the command to run, a man may experience his leg responding with a charley horse. In which case, aid is immediately sent to the hurting area. Relief begins the moment the muscles' unwanted activity ceases. The source of painful pressure is removed. The injured muscle is given an opportunity to "rest." Further relief may be administered by gently massaging the area of pain.

The Illustrated Manual of Nursing Practice[38] defines a massage as *a gentle yet firm handling of body parts for the purpose of helping circulation or to cause muscles to relax*. The application of the right amount and type of pressure encourages the distressed muscle's tension to be eased. After eliminating the sharp pain, moist penetrating heat or Ben Gay is often applied to encourage the aching in the muscle to lessen or cease altogether.

Sometimes, if the task originally attempted is still desired, a gentle stretching is added to the relief effort. It may even be added to the daily routine. This stretching often combines relief with conditioning so that the previously neglected muscle is able to perform the desired task(s) in the future.

I found it interesting that the nurse's manual instructs nurses not to massage inflamed areas. This is due to the risk of loosening of blood clots. If a blood clot should become dislodged, it could float to other areas and prohibit the normal flow of blood circulation, which can be fatal.

By the same token, when a wife has been given more responsibility than she can handle and she cries out, "I can't! This is too much!!," many a husband has insisted that it isn't

---

[38] Illustrated Manual of Nursing Practice, 4th Edition, 1991, Springhouse Corp., ISBN 0-87434-260-0

a matter of can't, but won't. He believes his wife is simply being stubborn. Instead of recognizing her as his adult equal, who is intimately familiar with her human limitations, he applies additional undue pressure by adding the heavier burden of guilt upon her. As he notices that the tasks he asks to be completed still do not get done, fury often results.

In his lack of understanding, he chooses not to favor his wife as he would his own body, by lessening the load. Instead, he increases her burden by speaking and thinking evil of her. Many wives respond with feelings of guilt. "Why can't I do what he asks of me? I try, but I feel so powerless to do anything he wants."

Husbands with a history of irresponsible behavior may interpret this response as defiance, selfishness, stupidity, and/or worthlessness. It isn't long before his behavior begins to reflect his thought life. This further compounds the problem because people *(in this case, wives)* tend to react negatively to demeaning behavior. Her negative reaction fosters his frustration. Hence, the Merry-Go-Round.

In the mind of the husband, the things he asks are simple. He doesn't grasp that the simplicity of the tasks requested is not the issue. The problem is that he has piled too much responsibility upon her. Oftentimes, an irresponsible man will *delegate* **his** responsibility to his wife. It doesn't matter to him that she is already overwhelmed by her failure to be "superwoman."

What do *you* do when your wife "cries out" in emotional pain? Many husbands continue to operate in ways that make their circumstances more painful for both them and their wives. To add insult to injury by virtue of their position of authority, they refuse to accept that their wife's disrespectful response(s) may be the fruit of neglect and/or abuse and little or no maintenance on their part. The necessary time, consistent care, and conditioning haven't been applied in the relationship. They are, in fact, reaping the harvest of neglect and abuse.

It is a fact of life that neglect and abuse breed deterioration. This deterioration in the marriage relationship has a direct impact on a wife's ability *(via overwhelming lack of motivation)* to respond with the respect and reverence her husband desperately needs and desires. Frequently, the husband is unaware that he is operating within the guidelines of a double standard. He ignores the concerns of his wife and plummets *(many times repetitiously)* headlong into relational bad backs, charley horses, muscle tears, and heart failures.

A husband who rejects his wife's attempts to confront him about irresponsible behavior negatively impacts harmony in the marriage. When he hasn't applied God's instruction to understand his wife and persists in rubbing his wife in areas where she is inflamed *(sensitive)*, he risks the danger of clots of disrespect dislodging and obstructing the flow of loving communication and intimacy between them. As a result, due to struggles with guilt about not respecting their husbands, some Christian wives experience physical, emotional, and/or spiritual breakdown.

In medical circumstances, blood-thinning medications are prescribed to dissolve blood clots. This brings us to the question, what "meds" has God prescribed for a husband to *dispense* to his wife in order to thin out the disrespect and irreverence that "clot" communication with his wife? What specifically can you do when you don't *know* what to do? If your marriage is *in pain*, one answer is to examine how you take care of *your own body* when it is in pain. Like the moist penetrating heat of Ben-Gay, consistent patience coupled with kindness has the ability to penetrate the tension between you and your wife when communication is *strained*. In 1 Corinthians 13, patience and kindness are the first attributes of love listed. The idea of patience here is not simply waiting until you get your way. It's a matter of being kind while you wait for the Lord to lead your next step.

The unique instruction to "love your wife *as your own body*" will yield great insight into specific application to problems between you and your spouse. Many times my husband and I have discussed how during times when we didn't really want to be bothered with each other, we both were lead to simply be kind towards each other. Thank God we were obedient to the Lord's leading! At times my husband's kindness toward me was as soothing as Ben-Gay on a sore muscle. It made him easier to talk with. *Aaaah!* ☺

Corporate vs. Organic Family Structure

One of the reasons a husband struggles with meeting the needs of his family may be due to the underlying perception he has of what his role in the family is. Often it is simply put, "I'm in charge." He sees his position in the home much like a corporation sees an organizational chart. He is at the top and everyone under his authority responds to him.

The problem inherent with this view is that often in a corporate environment, the one at the top has very little, if

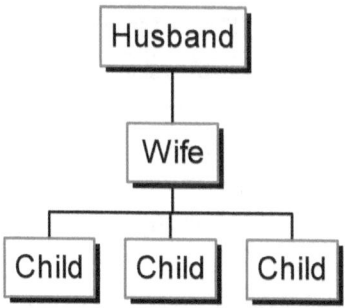

any, intimacy in his relationship with those under his authority. The one "in charge" may not even know what a subordinate's daily tasks require of them, or *know* who they are as persons. Many times, he doesn't care. As long as the deadlines and objectives he commands are carried out, he sees no reason to interact with those "under" him. Only when there is a problem does the one at the top get involved. Even then, he only gets involved when it is absolutely necessary. Furthermore, subordinates generate the source of provision and revenue.

By now, you may be thinking, "But somebody has to be *in charge*." If the man is the "head" of the family and the corporate organizational structure is inappropriate, what structure is appropriate?

In the Christian family, the source of provision is ordained to come *through* the "head." When viewing Christlike leadership, it could be said that the family organizational chart actually looks more like a tree.

The soil is the kingdom of God and all His righteousness. The husband acts as the root. The wife acts as the tree trunk, and the children are the branches. The character of each family member contributes to the quality of the fruit the family tree bears. Though structurally it appears that the husband is on the bottom *(last)*, the reality is that in order to provide spiritual and emotional nourishment for the family *(tree)* to thrive, the husband *(the root)* must *first be anchored* to a stable, nutrient-filled source of rich soil. The soil contains the things that will pertain to the life of the tree. The job of the roots is to tap into the nutrients in the soil.

Admittedly, there may not be much outside attention given to the husband. Very few people walk up to a beautiful fruit-bearing tree and say, "What a great root system this tree must have!" Nevertheless, the sweetness of the fruit and the beauty of the tree all speak to the effectiveness of the roots. If the root system is bad, the tree does not receive the proper nourishment to be fruitful. It's just a matter of time before the tree is cut down.

The dictionary's first definition of a root is;

- The underground part of a plant that serves as support, draws food and water from the surrounding soil, and stores food.

Its definition for the word rooted is;

- To become firmly settled, established, or entrenched.

As you will note, it is the responsibility of roots to not only provide nourishment, but also to support the tree *(stability),* and store up nourishment. There is a direct connection between the quality of the fruit and the root system's ability to provide the trunk and branches with what they need from the soil. When the roots sense that the surrounding soil doesn't have the water it needs for nourishment, it does not hopelessly and helplessly wish for rain. Nor does it go into denial or ignore the severity of its needs. It knows that the dryness of death in its branches is a call for help. It digs deeper into the soil searching for more nutrients and water. Were a husband to view his responsibility to his wife and family in this manner, the spirit of how he approached things would be very different. Instead of an attitude that expects others to serve him, the underlying belief would be one of service, like Christ.

My dear brother, I want to encourage you to pause for a moment. I realize that by now you may feel overwhelmed. If you are beginning to feel an acute sense of ineptness, relax. Our Father has provided for us. When we reach our limits, we can be honest with Him about how desperately we need Him.

At times, our lower nature seems hopelessly drawn toward an attitude of self-sufficiency. We know that "no man is an island," but in reality, our self-centeredness urges us to seek out methods that only serve to choke out God's truth in our hearts and minds. Sure, we know we are only human, but that doesn't build our SELF-esteem. As mortals, we are sometimes aggravated by our finiteness. We feel more comfortable with the masks we wear to hide our nagging sense of inadequacy. We don't dare let people see our imperfections. Underneath our masks, though, the thought of supplying someone else's nourishment may frighten us. We know how ill-equipped we are to meet the tasks. "If others find out what I'm really like, they'll never respect me." The self-gratifying attitudes of our culture and our masks couple like thieves, robbing us of our most precious possessions (*trust, respect, honor and love*) right from under our noses. So the masquerade continues.

But God our Father did not ask anything of His children for which He did not empower them. He has given us everything we need to rise to the challenges of life. Yes, learning God's way of relating *is* an awesome challenge. When He instructed His sons to love their wives as their own bodies, He gave them a precious tool. Prayerfully consider what the Lord has provided for you. Though He ultimately receives glory, honor, reverence, and admiration, He has given Himself as the premier example of servant leadership.

Some husbands/fathers insist on their loved ones being good *first* before they will be good to them. If the respect they desire isn't forthcoming, they become passive and refuse to become involved in the lives of their wife and children. Still other men demand what they want. Unwilling to admit the selfishness of their motives, they punish anyone who gets in the way of their goals. If this is how you have been, take this opportunity to repent of your failure to exhibit Christlike behavior.

The Bible says that we have all things that pertain unto life and godliness through the knowledge of Him who has called us to glory and valor.[39] As a Christian man, you have chosen the best place in the universe to anchor your family's tree. When you accepted Him as your Lord and Savior, He became the nutrient rich soil for you and your family to grow in. Christ's Spirit in you is able to help you accept the things you cannot change and the courage to change the things you can. By giving you His Spirit, He has already given you access to the wisdom necessary to know the difference.

If your lack of involvement in decision making, family, and marital intimacy has become a sensitive issue for you, please consider bringing "rest" to the aching in your marriage by making a deliberate effort to become more involved. Utilize the insight given in scripture. Be willing to prayerfully examine yourself and your motives. If you don't already have a trustworthy male friend you can talk this through with, ask God to send you one. He will.

---
[39] II Peter 1:3

In an earlier chapter I referred to the Biblical account of Balaam from Numbers 22. Stop now and take a moment to read it. Afterwards, ask the Lord Jesus to help you desire the truth as you answer the following questions:

- Have you continued to ask God about something(s) despite the fact that He has already told you what His *opposing* view is?

- Did you keep asking until God decided to "let you have it?"

- If so, are you so focused on what you want that you may be overlooking danger ahead?

- Do you feel injured by your wife's refusal to go the way you want to go?

- Does it seem like your plans to go in a certain direction are at a stand still because your wife has "fallen" beneath you?

- Have you been sensing the dryness of death in your relationships with family members?

- Have you responded to that dryness with demands or have you sought to provide spiritual and emotional nourishment for your family?

- Does your family have access to the richness of God through you? Or have you been a *bad root system*?

- Have you suffered pain from physical ailments? Could your response to that pain serve to enlighten you in how you could ease the pain in your relationship with your wife?

Prayerfully meditate on these questions. Consider your answers. Notice the thoughts and emotions that surface in your mind. Are they self-centered? Angry? If so, what are you really angry about? As the answers come to your mind, even if it's an embarrassing mess, take it all to our Father. Know that just as He was there when Abraham, Moses, David, John, Peter, and Paul struggled, He is there for you. He'll give you courage to leave the familiar behavior patterns that rob you so that you can step out into the unknown yet rewarding life of trusting Him.

Dear Father,

Thank You for my brother's desire to know the truth. Help him as he makes efforts to love his wife as his own body. If he has any physically weak areas in his body, help him see the connection between his tender responses to his body when it's in pain versus the responses he gives his mate when their relationship is struggling. If he is neglectful of his body, help him to see that just as his health is deteriorating without care, so will his communication and relationship with his wife. May he draw closer to You in the process. Amen.

13. How to Recognize an Irresponsible Man

"Girl, if a man wants me in his life, he'd better have a car, a house, nice clothes, and a good job. Otherwise, I won't give him the time of day."

As a young woman, when I heard other females make these comments, I dismissed them as too materialistic. They seemed more concerned about what they could get out of the relationship from a materialistic standpoint than what they could bring to the relationship so it could last a lifetime. I personally was more concerned with whether or not the man and I were *in love*. It never dawned on me that, despite the materialistic tone of their comments, their point of view still contained something of value to consider.

Possession of these things could be evidence that he has enough self-discipline in his character to set goals and diligently work to obtain them. How he maintains his possessions can also be observed. If he owns a car, is it kept in proper repair? Are his clothes clean? Does he keep himself clean? Is he faithful in going to church and work? Is his house or apartment taken care of? Positive answers to these questions are no guarantee that you have found the "perfect" husband. However, it does give you some insight into some of what you can expect should you marry him. If the things he possesses are properly maintained, it is a relatively safe assumption that he will continue to do so after he his married.

I imagine there are young women reading this book who are swooning romantics like I was *(am?)*. I knew single men who didn't have any of those things. Yet, I considered them to be sincere believers, as well as all around "nice" people. In fact, I considered myself to be a "nice" person.

Life before Christ can leave a person's life a total mess. Many believers truly understand what it means for God to give you a chance to "start over." In fact, when I met my husband, neither of us had all those things. Why require someone to have something you don't even possess?

If the man you love doesn't have these things, it doesn't mean you should immediately dismiss him out of your life. It does mean that you need to consider what his attitude is regarding self-discipline and work ethic and whether or not you are willing to live with what you see after thorough observation.

If he isn't working, you need to know why. You may want to ask where he has worked and how long he was there. You would do well to make a mental note if his reason(s) for leaving his job(s) seem to always be someone else's fault. Unfortunately, some men develop a pattern of hopping from job to job never knowing what their gifts are or establishing roots anywhere because they have difficulty being under authority. If this is the case with your potential mate, you may want to make it a point to observe how he handles himself when *he* is the one with authority. Is he approachable? Can he handle others disagreeing with him? How does he handle *you* disagreeing with him?

For a very young man under 21 trying to find his niche in life, I suppose it could be considered somewhat "normal" to job-hop. But when a man is over 21 years old, with no job, not pursuing any type of education or training, living *off* mom or some one else and little or no personal possessions to speak of, let the red lights flash and the sirens blare. Do not allow your head to be filled with romantic notions. That man is behaving irresponsibly.

Please note that I chose to phrase my statement "living *off*" mom as opposed to "living *with*" mom. I personally do not believe it is automatically a sign of irresponsibility for a man to be living with his mother if he is unmarried, especially if she is elderly. The crime rate being what it is today, a man may very well live with his mother as a way of protecting her while providing financial stability for both of them *(notice he is doing the providing)*. However, if he is an able bodied, relatively intelligent man who doesn't work and contribute to the household he lives in, whether he lives with his mother or some other relative, that brother's behavior is irresponsible.

One pastor told me how saddened he was by the reality that many of the young women in his congregation who desire to marry claim to have never met an *available* man who has a car, and/or a house, nice clothes, and a job where he earns wages honestly. I have even heard that some women have never seen an *available* man who has acquired anything. How sad.

* * *

Some women currently married to men who behave irresponsibly would tell us that the desire to be loved can create an emotional vacuum that aches so badly that women rush into marriage without examining the character of the man they *love*. During courtship they recognized their mate's irresponsible behavior. Unfortunately, the dread they experienced at the thought of being alone coupled with an intense longing for companionship caused their emotions to rule out good judgment.

You can obtain wisdom from their hindsight by not even allowing yourself the opportunity to *fall in love* by recognizing irresponsible behavior before you even consider dating a man. By refusing to spend time alone with men until you have observed whether or not they possess the character becoming a friend, much less a marriage partner, you will likely avoid the heartache of these types of relationships altogether.

Don't allow the voice of loneliness to cry out in desperation, "Will somebody, anybody, love me?" Trust me ladies, there is a huge difference between a man who *has* character, and a man who *is a* character. This is an opportunity to realize that God's Word is true or it isn't. Our Father has said that He "will *never* forsake us." That means we are never alone.

Still other women are already engaged and have never been treated with kindness. They swallow whole anything that looks and feels better than the neglect or abuse they're accustomed to. Unfortunately, everything with bubbles isn't champagne. If you are single and the man you love has patterns of irresponsibility, DO NOT overlook it. By utilizing the information provided in this book, you may be instrumental in his facing the truth about his behavior before you get married and avoid the Merry-Go-Round altogether.

* * *

I believe a good way to increase our understanding of how to recognize a man who behaves irresponsibly, is by first defining terms. The prefix "ir" before the word "responsibility" communicates that there is an absence or lack of the ability to be responsible. Webster defines responsible as:

1 a : liable to be called on to answer

b 1: liable to be called to account as the primary cause, motive, or agent (a committee *responsible* for the job)

b 2: being the cause or explanation (mechanical defects were *responsible* for the accident)

c : liable to legal review or in case of fault to penalties

2 a : able to answer for one's conduct and obligations : <u>Trustworthy</u>

b : able to choose for oneself between right and wrong

A wise woman can evaluate her potential mate's behavior by holding it up to the true meaning of the word for comparison and ask herself the following questions:

1. Is my future mate willing to answer for his behavior when he is called upon to do so? Or does he tend to become angry when his behavior is in question?

2. Is he willing to give an account as the primary cause, motive, or agent regarding matters of importance as a good leader would? Or does he pass the buck and cast blame?

3. Is he trustworthy? Or do you find it difficult to believe the things he tells you?

4. Does he choose for himself between right and wrong? Or does he *need you* to keep him out of trouble.

If you find that he is unable to do these things, you need to re-evaluate things and ask yourself:

- Do I want to marry someone who is too immature to admit when he makes mistakes?
- Do I want a spouse who becomes angry when I ask him questions? Especially questions about things that are important to our family and me?
- Do I want a husband who "delegates" his responsibility to me so I can be the heavy if things don't work out?
- Do I want a mate who I have to second guess or wonder about things he says because he has shown himself to be untrustworthy?
- Do I want the man I marry to be a lifetime adult companion or a childlike adult I have to look after?

The answers to these questions may help you cut through the haze of *being in love* long enough to thoroughly think things through. Marriage was designed to be a lifetime commitment. As such, one needs to consider what kinds of behavior issues you will be addressing for the rest of your life.

The Scripture encourages us to provoke each other to love and good works.[40] By applying the principles outlined in this book, you *may* be able to provoke your future mate into love and good works *before* the wedding. But consider yourself warned. There are no promises. You cannot change anyone.

Make sure that "Ms. I'm So Lonely" is not picking out your husband. Exercise wisdom. You may need to let this time in your life be an opportunity for the Holy Spirit to bear the fruit of patience in your walk with the Father.

Make sure that you diligently seek the Lord before marrying a man. God has called husbands to be lovers, providers, protectors, and leaders in their homes. Pray diligently and sincerely seek an answer from God. Ask others to pray with you

---

[40] Hebrews 10:24

that God will confirm whether or not He has chosen the man you're interested in to be *the* one to love, provide for, protect, and lead you for the rest of your life. Don't make a lifetime decision without having counted the costs and obtained insight from God's Word. After all, He knows you both, better than anyone.

And ladies, since the scripture instructs us to take the log out of own eye first, don't forget to ask yourself these questions. It's always good to possess the qualities you're looking for.

Dear Father,

As a single woman, help me to trust You in selecting my mate. At times I feel so lonely that I may not remember that You see me as a whole person who is complete in You.

Cause me to possess the things I am looking for in a mate. When a young man catches my eye, help me to pause long enough to see if he has allowed You to capture his heart. Help me to trust You with all matters concerning selecting a mate.

*If You have chosen that I am to have a "single" life, help me to **know** and accept it so that I don't waste time yearning for something I will never have. Help me to recognize that even if You give me a mate, he is to never become more important to me than You! Amen.*

14. Jump Recovery

If you've ever watched a child jump or fall off a Merry-Go-Round, you've seen that depending on how fast the ride was going, and what part of the body hit the ground first, there is a delay in time between hitting the ground and getting up. I call this time delay, "jump recovery." If you've stayed in the process thus far, despite all the things you have suffered, you have courageously "jumped" away from things that displease God, into the pain of landing on the hard ground of truth. It hurts. You're not sure how badly you are injured. As you go to "get up," everything aches. You know you'll have to move slowly. At times you may even wonder if you have a concussion or if you'll ever "walk" again. Despair may hound you as you realize that you just need to lie still – and wait until you feel strong enough to move.

We live in a culture that abhors patience. Everything that isn't done in microseconds is dismissed as obsolete. That simply is not so with our Father. To the dismay of many, patience is a necessity in the kingdom of God.

When I encountered the "jump recovery" stage, I "laid on the ground" a long time. I was bruised and in excruciating pain. When others came, attempting to "help me up" they tried to move me a lot quicker than I was able to move. My emotional "bones" ached so badly that I wasn't sure I hadn't "broken" something. At times I wasn't sure if I hadn't become completely paralyzed. In my heart I knew "jumping" had been the right decision. Yet, I struggled with how something *right* could feel so *bad*.

Unable to "get up" I realized that I simply had to lie there. I'd either wait until I received enough strength, or I'd wait for the paramedics. Disappointed with the response of church leaders, I lost interest in going to church. I prayed. I read Scripture and meditated. To keep from becoming isolated and removed from godly influence, I made sure I met often with friends who desire to live out God's truth. For months I deliberately did not minister or attend regular worship services. I also withdrew emotionally from my husband. I had taught him that my love demonstrated itself in pacifying and controlling. Having decided to "pluck up" the unhealthy responses I planted, I was trying to relate differently. But, I didn't know how to act. At times, leaving him felt like the best thing. Truthfully it was just the easiest thing. A couple of times I was so angry I told him I was "just barely there." He was in such misery he didn't care. In fact, he welcomed the thought.

Eventually, I'd been out of church so long my then 16-year-old daughter, Elayna, said, "Mom are you okay? I'm worried that you're not going to church. You're a minister. What kind of example are you setting for your children?" What won't we try to do for our children? In my heart I felt a little strength stirring. Everything still ached but somehow I was determined to "get up."

I began visiting other churches. Having discerned the calling God had given my husband and me, various church leaders encouraged us to become involved in their ministries. When my husband found one he liked, I began attending services with him. The services were energetic. The people were energetic, kind, and thoughtful. I felt welcomed. As time passed, the weight of responsibility was placed upon my shoulders at a time when the weight of a struggling marriage had not been completely lifted. A part of me wanted so much to reach out and minister. Another part of me was simply not willing to return to what appeared to be a whirlwind of *religious* activity.

Over time I began to feel like I was returning to the masquerade ball that I promised myself I wouldn't go to. Something inside me screamed, "I won't do it! No!!! I will not wear a mask again!" Be courteous, yes. Be considerate of other's feelings, absolutely. Be a phony, no way!

Sadly, I lost interest in going to church again. Thankfully, this time around I was able to experience sadness without a lot of complaining. I simply chose to rest in the arms of the Master. At times my family was amazed at how much I lost interest in attending worship services. I know it was rooted in not feeling strong enough to handle the pressure of explaining to concerned, well meaning believers why I wasn't ready to get involved with various activities.

This time as I lay on the hard ground of the truth it came to me. Jesus is the truth! I may feel weak and unable to move, but if I am surrounded by truth my Heavenly Father surrounds me. I took comfort in the knowledge that He had me in His arms. He held me. He accepted me. He nourished me. He tended my wounds. He comforted me. He strengthened me. He talked with me. He tended my wounds and He held me some more. He allowed me to sit in His lap bruised and confused, but mending.

As I rested in His arms, we talked about my future. He clarified things for me and brought them into clearer focus. Inside I felt things stabilizing. I had more resolve in my mind. As I made decisions, I noticed I was becoming firmer in the courage of my convictions. It was so nice in "Abba's" lap. I sensed that He was content to let me take my time and rest from *my labor.* I was content to sit here. I got pretty banged up when I jumped off my Merry-Go-Round. I have the scars to prove it.

As I spent time recovering from my "jump," I sensed genuine confidence increasing inside me. Fear was dissipating. I saw myself becoming a woman of courage. How? When? I tried for years to feel this confident, *be* this confident. Was it going through the pain? Was it the self-examination? Was it what I said? Was it what I did?

It took me a while to realize that it wasn't making the decision to stop enabling my husband, though that helps. It wasn't the self-examination, though that is important. It wasn't implementing and maintaining responsible behavior patterns for myself, though I desperately needed to do those things. It wasn't sharing my pain with others, though that was incredibly valuable. After prayerful thinking and reading and studying it finally dawned on me. In the midst of all the madness and darkness, I was closer to my Father than ever before. He was allowing me to *know* Him better. Get closer to Him. The confidence and courage started coming when I began to truly notice:

- How patient He is.

- How merciful He is.

- How humorous He can be.

- How kind and gentle He is.

- How wonderful He is.

- How sweet talking with Him is.

- How constant His love for me is.

- How He was empowering me to increase in these aspects of His character.

The tenderness, intimacy, stability, and protection I tried to pry from my husband through the years I received from the one who loved me first and best. What a joy! It changed our whole relationship.

Before, in my relationship with God, I spent much of my time checking to make sure I was doing things "right." Although I understood that I couldn't earn my way to heaven, I was so grateful for His goodness toward me that I never wanted to be a source of disappointment to Him.

Consequently, my vision was so heavily focused on "doing the right thing" that I missed the point. Like the husband mentioned earlier, I was poised to swat anything in my life that was unlike God. How ridiculous! I would have spent my entire life swatting. Where would the joy have been in that? Suddenly, truth has come bursting through. All this time I had blamed my husband for being the reason my joy was gone. But it wasn't him at all. It was my own self-centered desire for my husband, my children, and my life to be perfect. How utterly foolish of me! I am human. Everyone I love is human. Until Christ returns and changes us, none of us will ever be perfect. *[Daaa!]* ☺

As important as doing things right is, it is not the thing to focus my life on. The focal point of my life should be, *knowing* Him. To *know* God is to invite the most awesome light into the dark places of your heart. Because evil thrives in dark places, the presence of God's light compels the darkness to flee and the shackles of sin to lose their grip. It is written, that where the Spirit of the Lord is, there is liberty.[41]

---
[41] II Corinthians 3:17

In the midst of a horrible season of situations, I was set free from the need to be what others expected instead of who I was.

It is also written that in His presence there is fullness of joy.[42] Not the kind of joy I had before that made me sing, dance, shout, and testify *(although these things are good)*. This joy runs deeper. It's like a huge, bright and beaming smile at the core of my being, where there had once been a frown.

I am looking forward to spending more time getting to know Him. Because I'm still dealing with the repercussions of *my* irresponsible choices, I'm sure there will be lots of opportunity to get closer to Him. As I continue my efforts to correct the things I've done wrong, finish paying the folks I owe, and not make irresponsible, fearful decisions, it is so comforting to know that my heavenly Father is with me. I *know* for myself that God accepts me.

In the past when I went to *spend time* with God, I always had an agenda. I wanted Him to *give me* relief when the pain of life seemed unbearable. I wanted Him to *give me* a dynamic message so I could impress people. I wanted Him to *give me* His stamp of approval when I ran my ideas past Him. I wanted Him to *give me* wisdom so I could help my loved ones when they were in distress. But as I experience *being with Him*, I realize that I genuinely enjoy just being around Him.

In my heart *He is* more than just the awesome, majestic, omnipotent, omniscient, dependable Creator. *He is* my friend. I know now that as fantastic as it is to be able to depend on His greatness, it is even more wonderful to just hang out with Him 'cause *He is* such a pleasure to be with. *He is* a great guy! ☺

When you enter the "jump recovery" stage battered, bruised, and wounded from jumping off the Merry-Go-

---

[42] Psalm 16:11

Round onto the hard ground of the truth, just lie there. Know that you are in His arms. Let Him hold you. Tend your wounds. Strengthen you. Comfort you and hold you some more. Don't be in a hurry. Take your time. Let Him talk with you about your past, present, and future. Enjoy your contact with Him. Ultimately *knowing* Him will give you the courage to get up from the ground and walk away from the Merry-Go-Round knowing that the same God who loves you, also loves your mate. Whether or not your mate continues riding the Merry-Go-Round is not your decision. God has given him the right to choose. So remember, that choice is up to him.

In conclusion, you may have lost the respect *of* your husband, just as you lost respect *for* him. However, as you spend time with God the reality of your association with Him will become more apparent. Instead of being a façade you wear, courage and joy, love and patience will become a part of who you are. This is *real* virtue. Today the word means moral excellence. To be certain a Christian woman definitely wants to be morally excellent. But if we were to restate the verse with its original intent it would say,

A woman with the courage and valor of a man who can find? Her worth is considered to be far greater than that of rubies.

A courageous person tends to have the respect of all that know them. In the marriage setting, where a wife is confident and not afraid with any amazement, her husband *(if he genuinely loves her)* will eventually hold much respect for his courageous wife. He knows that she will not permit him to defile her life with ungodly behavior. Yet, he becomes grateful because her strength is truly *help* in moments when his ability to resist evil is weak or under attack.

Though she is submissive to his God-ordained authority, she does not grant his every whim. Because she will not try to manipulate or control him in any way, he senses that his wife is not threatened by the freedom he has to be whoever he is. In fact, somehow she celebrates it. A truly virtuous *(courageous)* Christian wife speaks God's truth in love and does not waver when her husband expresses displeasure. By sharing her heart and releasing him to make whatever decisions he wants and allowing him to experience the repercussions of his actions, she shows a great deal of respect for her husband. By maintaining her convictions she shows genuine virtue *(courage and moral excellence)*, trust, confidence in God, and respect for herself. This woman has the liberty of Christ to be who she is. Her courageous and wise behavior is so apparent that her husband and children call her blessed. By the power of God's Spirit, this woman is you.

Stop and think about all you have faced on our journey together through the pages of this book. You have gone into the dark places of your heart, repented of your lack of confidence in God, and chosen to turn from your own wickedness. You have stood firm in the face of vehement displays of anger from your loved ones and said "no" to ungodly things you know just months, weeks, and days ago you would have relinquished. When fear dogged your steps, you took authority over yourself and refrained from contributing to the unhealthy behavior cycles of the past. You have embraced the love of your Savior and remained committed to *truly knowing* and worshipping Him amidst ridicule from those who don't understand. Your husband knows that you respect him so much that you are going to let him prove his own work so he can have confidence in his God given ability to accomplish things (Galatians 6:4). You know that as you continue to live for Christ you will recommit to any and all these decisions as often as necessary.

In the future, as you go through various emotional battlefields, the weapons you use are not unhealthy, cowardly responses. Your weaponry is mighty through God.

It pulls down every stronghold and casts down every imagination in your life that would stand up against the *know*ledge of our Lord Jesus *Christ.* You are determined to possess the abundant life He promised those who believe in Him. The gifts and talents given you by the Father are under the guidance and direction of His Spirit, where there is authentic freedom. When life's problems cause you to feel puny and weak, you will draw from the wellspring of your faith in God who has told us that *no weapon formed against us shall prosper.*[43] You will take authority over your fears and stand fighting the good fight of faith. In so doing you bear yet another fruit of the Holy Spirit, temperance, by controlling the only one you *can* control – you.

***

Best of all, not only does God know you – you *know Him.*

---

[43] Isaiah 54:17

Recommended Reading

Classic resources informed this work. Though the dates of these publications may seem outdated to some, the truths they reveal are timeless.

1. Beattie, Melody, *Beyond Codependency and Getting Better All the Time* (New York: Hazelden Foundation, 1989)
2. Beattie, Melody, *Codependency No More: How to Stop Controlling Others and Start Caring for Yourself* (New York: Hazelden Foundation, 1987, 1992)
3. Chapman, Gary, *The Five Love Languages: How to Express Heartfelt Commitment to Your Mate* (Chicago, IL: Northfield Publishing, 1992)
4. Chapman, Gary, *Wounded Marriages Can Be Healed: Hope for the Separated* (Chicago, IL: Moody Press, 1996)
5. Christenson, Evelyn, *Lord Change Me* (Colorado Springs, CO: Chariot Victor Publishing, 1993)
6. Cloud, Henry and Townsend, John, *Boundaries in Marriage* (Grand Rapids, MI: Zondervan, 1999)
7. Cloud, Henry and Townsend, John, *Boundaries: When to Say Yes and When to Say No to Take Control of Your Life* (Grand Rapids, MI: Zondervan, 1993)
8. Cloud, Henry and Townsend, John, *Changes That Heal* (Grand Rapids, MI: Zondervan, 1996)
9. Cloud, Henry and Townsend, John, *Twelve "Christian" Beliefs That Can Drive You Crazy: Relief from False Assumptions* (Grand Rapids, MI: Zondervan, 1994, 1995)
10. Cole, Ed, *Communication, Sex and Money* (Tulsa, OK: Honor Books, 1987)

11. Cole, Ed, *Courage: Winning Life's Toughest Battles* (Tulsa, OK: Honor Books, 1985, 1991)

12. Cole, Ed, *Facing the Challenge of Crisis and Change* (Tulsa, OK: Honor Books, 1993)

13. Cole, Ed, *Maximized Manhood: A Guide to Family Survival* (Springdale, PA: Whitaker House, 1982)

14. Crabb, Lawrence *Connecting: Healing Ourselves and Our Relationships, A Radical New Vision* (Nashville, TN: Word Publishing, 1997)

15. Crabb, Lawrence *Real Change is Possible: If You're Willing to Start from the Inside Out* (Colorado Springs, CO: Navpress, 1988)

16. Crabb, Lawrence, *Hope When You're Hurting* (Grand Rapids, MI: Zondervan, 1996)

17. Crabb, Lawrence, *Understanding Who You Are: What Your Relationships Tell You About Yourself* (Colorado Springs, CO: Navpress, 1997)

18. Dobson, James *Love Must Be Tough: New Hope for Families in Crisis* (Dallas, TX: Word Publishing, 1993, 1996)

19. Forward, Susan and Torres, Joan, *Men Who Hate Women and the Women Who Love Them: When Loving Hurts and You Don't Know Why* (New York: Bantam Books, 1986)

20. Groom, Nancy *From Bondage to Bonding: Escaping Codependency, Embracing Biblical Love* (Colorado Springs, CO: Navpress, 1991)

21. Groom, Nancy *Married Without Masks, A New Look at Submission and Authority* (Grand Rapids: Baker Book House Company, 1996)

22. Leman, Kevin, *Pleasers: Women Who Can't Say No and the Men Who Control Them* (Old Tappan, NJ: Fleming H. Revell Co., 1987)

23. Lepine, Bob, *The Christian Husband: God's Vision of Loving and Caring for Your Wife* (Ann Arbor, MI: Servant Publications, 1999)

24. Nair, Ken *The Key to Becoming a Strong and Irresistible Husband is, Discovering the Mind of a Woman* (Nashville, TN: Thomas Nelson Publishers, 1995)

25. Norwood, Robin, *Women Who Love Too Much: When You Keep Wishing and Hoping He'll Change* (Pocket Books : St. Martin's Press, 1985)

26. Olsen, Kathy, *Silent Pain: Finding God's Comfort for Your Hidden Heartaches* (Colorado Springs, CO: Navpress, 1992)

27. Roberts, Lee *Praying God's Will for My Husband* (Nashville, TN: Nelson Publishers, 1993)

28. Rosberg, Gary, *Choosing to Love Again* (Colorado Springs, CO: Focus on the Family Publishing, 1992)

29. Smalley, Gary and Trent, John *The Gift of Blessing* (New York: Inspirational Press, 1986)

30. Smalley, Gary and Trent, John *The Gift of Honor* (New York: Inspirational Press, 1987)

31. Swindoll, Charles R., *Improving Your Serve* (Nashville, TN: Word Publishing, 1997)

32. Swindoll, Charles R., *Living Above the Level of Mediocrity* (Anaheim, CA: Insight For Living, 1997)

33. Swindoll, Charles R., *Stress Fractures: Biblical Splints for Every Day Pressures* (Portland, OR: Multnomah, 1990)

34. Swindoll, Charles R., *Strike the Original Match* (Wheaton, IL: Tyndale House Publishers, 1990)

35. Swindoll, Charles, *Encourage Me: Caring Words for Heavy Hearts* (Grand Rapids, MI: Zondervan, 1982)

36. Townsend, John, *Hiding from Love: How to change the Withdrawal Patterns that Isolate and Imprison You* (Colorado Springs, CO: Navpress, 1991)

37. Wardle, Terry, *Wounded: How You Can Find Inner Wholeness and Healing in Him* (Harrisburg, PA: Christian Publications, 1994)

About the Author

Christina Dixon is a truth-teller and tender-hearted guide for those navigating the complicated terrain of family estrangement, reconciliation, and emotional healing. A dynamic speaker, author, podcast host, and book coach, she draws on her faith, experience, and education to help others rebuild what was broken, reclaim their voice, and walk with integrity through life's most difficult chapters.

Her willingness to name the uncomfortable: that guilt can't be the glue that holds a family together. That love without accountability is dangerous. That presence without emotional availability isn't enough. And that restoration, real restoration, isn't a one-time moment—it's a process. A journey. A daily decision to show up with truth and tenderness, even when it's easier to hide behind excuses or spiritual platitudes.

For more than two decades, Christina has been encouraging and equipping others through her work as a speaker, writer, and coach. She is the author of the widely shared book *How to Respect an Irresponsible Man*, a bold and insightful resource that challenges traditional narratives around relationships and respect. She is also the coauthor of *HELP! For Your Leadership, African American Church Leadership,* and the visionary publisher behind PriorityONE Publications, a growing library of resources for people committed to providing emotional honesty, personal growth, and spiritual maturity.

Her publishing and coaching business has served aspiring authors, public figures, ministers, and everyday individuals looking to tell their stories with courage and clarity. Whether ghostwriting memoirs, editing life-changing books, or preparing authors for launch, Christina combines technical excellence with deep compassion. Her mission is simple: to help people speak, write, and live with courage—on the page, on the mic, and in their daily lives.

Christina's tagline, "Speaking, Writing, and Coaching to Encourage, Challenge, and Inspire YOU!" perfectly captures her approach. She believes in grace, but not in skipping the growth that grace calls us to. That's why both conviction and compassion mark her speaking, books, and coaching.

Christina serves her community as the Women's Ministry President at her local church, New Hope Progressive Church of Christ (Holiness) USA, where her husband, Elder Michael Dixon, is the pastor. In the recent past, she served as Chair of the Board of Directors for the International Christian Education Association, and Board Member for the Readers Become Leaders Literacy Agency and Book Club, as well as former President of the United Christian Women's Ministries for Michigan/Ohio District and former Vice Chair of the Marriage Resource Center.

As a wife, mother of five, grandmother of five, and spiritual mentor to many, Christina carries a multi-generational passion for healing. She believes that the choices we make today—especially the honest ones—can change the legacy we leave tomorrow.

Christina and her husband live in Detroit, Michigan.

For more information or to book Mrs. Dixon for speaking engagements, or radio and television interviews, contact:
PriorityONE Publications, LLC
ATTN: Christina Dixon
P. O. Box 361332, Grosse Pointe, MI 48236
Email requests to: info@christinadixon.net
Website - http://www.christinadixon.net

Book Order Form

How to Respect an Irresponsible Man!
By Christina Dixon

Name _____

Address _____

City _____ State _____ Zip _____

Phone _____ Fax _____

Email _____

Quantity	
Price *(each)*	$14.99
Subtotal	
S & H *(each)*	$3.99
MI Tax 6%	
TOTAL	

METHOD OF PAYMENT:

☐ Check or Money Order
(*Make payable to*: **Christina Dixon**)

☐ Visa   ☐ Master Card   ☐ Discover   ☐ American Express

Acct No. _____

Expiration Date (*mmyy*) _____

Signature _____

Mail your payment with this form to:
PriorityONE Publications, LLC
ATTN: Christina Dixon
P. O. Box 361332
Grosse Pointe, MI 48236
(313) 312-5318 – Southeast Michigan
URL: http://www.christinadixon.net
Email: info@christinadixon.net

www.ingramcontent.com/pod-product-compliance
Lightning Source LLC
Chambersburg PA
CBHW031251290426
44109CB00012B/537